Marilyn

How to Eat Out in France

How to understand the menu and make yourself understood

Dictionary and Phrase Book for the Restaurant

GREMESE

Originally published as:
La Francia al Ristorante

© 1996 L'Airone Editrice
P.O.Box 14237
00149 Rome – Italy

English translation:
Sandra Tokunaga

Jacket design:
Carlo Soldatini

Photocomposition:
Graphic Art 6 s.r.l. – Rome

Printed and bound by:
ARTI GRAFICHE LA MODERNA – Roma – Italy

© 1997 Gremese International s.r.l.
P.O. Box 14335
00149 Rome – Italy

ISBN 88-7301-098-9

Just say "France," and the exquisite pleasures of its table invariably come to mind – the studied refinement that makes French gastronomy so special, its host of illustrious wines adored the world over. Indeed, it is no secret to anyone that the French love to eat, and above all, to eat well.

So, won't you join us? Accept this invitation to explore all the subtle blends, delicate aromas, intricate tastes – bound to be as much a feast for the eyes as for the palate – of one of the world's most celebrated cuisines.

For those who want to make their stay in France more than just the superficial visit of the unprepared traveler, this guide hopes to provide many of the precious insights of the discerning connoisseur, who knows just what to select and how to appreciate the very best wherever he goes.

In these pages you will find a vast overview of French cuisine with many of its most characteristic dishes and products listed in alphabetical order and described simply and clearly. There is also a handy section with all of those useful words and phrases so vital to understanding others and making yourself understood, particularly in restaurants.

A selection of some of the most typically French recipes is also included to make it easy, once back home, to repeat those dishes which have become your favorites in France (particularly if you've had the chance to pick up some local products) and will be a wonderful way to relive some of the nicest moments of your holiday.

Although our guide certainly does not claim to cover everything there is to know about the culture of a country so very rich in tradition and history, we would nevertheless like to warmly wish you "Bon Appétit!" as you set off to discover, through the French and their food, the art and pleasure of living in France.

INTRODUCTION

MEALS IN FRANCE

The typical French meal is decidedly long and copious and
consists of numerous courses, each one complemented by a
different wine.
You begin with an *apéritif:* an alcoholic beverage served with
appetizers to nibble such as savory biscuits, olives, puff
pastry canapés or tiny toasts garnished in an infinite number
of festive ways.
The actual meal often begins with a *potage* (soup) served in
place of, or following, an hors-d'oeuvre which might be any
type of opener from a salad garnished with fish, shellfish or
giblets, to a selection of patés or cold cuts, not to mention, of
course, the exquisite delicacy *foie gras.* There usually follow
two "main courses." The first will most likely be fish, but
may sometimes be snails or perhaps frogs legs served in a
delicate sauce.
By the time you get to the halfway point of one of these
particularly abundant meals, you will probably welcome the
short break the French have called *trou normand*, during
which they sit back and sip a glass of Calvados to digest the
first part of the meal, or to re-awaken the appetite and
sharpen the tastebuds for the courses to follow. The *trou
normand* might also appear in the more elaborate form of a
cup of apple sherbet doused with Calvados, or lemon sherbet
floating in champagne.
Thus restored, you will be presented with the "second" main
course which will probably consist of a platter of meat or
game with a helping of cooked vegetables on the side. A
tossed green salad will then follow, and after that, a generous
and artfully presented cheeseboard, to complete the "savory"
part of the meal.
Clearly this type of menu is reserved for special occasions.
On ordinary days, the French will prefer an abbreviated form

usually consisting of a soup or other starter, then a main course of either fish or meat and a side dish of cooked vegetables, and finally, the normal green salad, cheese and dessert.

RESTAURANTS IN FRANCE

In this land of "restaurants on every corner" you will probably be pleasantly surprised to discover that there are many places where you can have a very satisfying meal without spending a fortune – beginning with the restaurant in your own hotel which should offer at least this, if not more, depending, of course, on the overall standing of the hotel itself. Nevertheless, the best way to really get to know French cooking, is to seek out the traditional restaurants where the widest choice of local gastronomic specialties will be offered.

There will be many tempting up-market restaurants particularly in the big cities and resort areas. These will propose either a highly refined style of cooking inspired by the now famous *nouvelle cuisine*, or else dishes more staunchly attached to traditional roots but "lightened up" in conformity with the sensible dictates of modern dietetics. In these restaurants the wine list is generally excellent and a selection of the finest products of national renown are reserved for its patrons. If you decide to try one of these two types of restaurants, it is always best to reserve.

The last point concerns prices, which will almost always be displayed outside the restaurant itself and, of course, will reflect the overall standard of the establishment and the quality of its menu. On the whole, though, most restaurants propose a varied menu and pleasant atmosphere at quite reasonable prices.

For those who really want to be sure not to spend too much, however, the best solution still remains the fixed-price menu. Almost all restaurants propose a minimum of two types of these set menus with a choice between two first courses, two main courses, and then cheese and/or fruit, thus offering the attractive advantage of sampling local specialties at limited cost. Very often wine is not included in the price of the menu (except for the local house wine), but bread, water and service are. You will always find the applied percentage for service indicated on the menu. It is also recommended in this type of establishment to reserve, though it is not absolutely indispensable.

Other than the traditional-type restaurants described above, there also exist a variety of original little places that specialize in specific types of food, such as *crêperies*, that offer a long list of different types of sweet and savory crêpes, or oyster bars, or *saladeries* (salad bars) or, finally, places where you may spend a unique evening, for example, having only cheese in all forms imaginable.

If you are in somewhat of a hurry, you can always grab a quick bite at a *bistrot* or go into a *brasserie*, which is a large café that also serves hot meals. As cafés still remain the hub of street life, particularly in the big cities, *brasseries* are almost always buzzing with activity and interesting people in a congenial atmosphere.

As we leave the city for the countryside, places called *relais* will start appearing along the way, where anything from a light snack to a full banquet may be requested. You will also begin spotting many *auberges*, types of local inns that offer traditional cuisine, perhaps a bit more country-style than city restaurants, but just as carefully prepared and delicious.

In the southwest region of France, it is common to find charming little places called *guinguette* in picturesque settings along river banks where you can dine and dance away long summer evenings and spend surprisingly very little. Still far from the big city, you will also find little restaurants called *routiers* along the itineraries of truck driver regulars who stop there, well-briefed on where they can count on a reasonably priced, hearty and tasty meal. To complete this general overview of restaurants in France, we might also mention the so-called *restauroutes*: large cafeteria-style restaurants situated conveniently along all major highways. There will also be self-service restaurants in most large shopping centers for quick and inexpensive meals. At any rate, before deciding on where to go, be sure to consult the menu and prices which, as mentioned before, are almost always displayed outside the door.

As regards payment, most restaurants accept major credit cards, particularly in the larger cities and tourist spots. Prices, of course, vary with the type of restaurant, but the average cost for a full meal should come to about 100 to 150 Francs per person, though there will be lots of places where you can have a very good meal for much less. Although service is included in the bill, it is nevertheless customary to leave the waiter a tip of about 10 Francs, or in any case, a tip in proportion to the bill. One last point to note, about opening hours: restaurants are generally open for lunch from noon until 2:30 P.M. and for dinner from 7:30 P.M. until 10:30 P.M., bearing in mind that these hours might vary slightly depending on the region and the season.

The production of sweets is particularly developed in all regions and the list that follows will include those most widely available – the absolute "musts" to try.

Bouchon bordelais: A cork-shaped piece of chocolate with a cocoa and liqueur filling.

Calisson d'Aix: Cookie with an almond-paste filling, covered with sugar icing. Specialty from Aix-en-Provence.

Dragée: Almond or hazel nut covered with sugar icing.

Fruits déguisés: Small fruit covered in sugar or in almond paste; or almond paste in the shape of fruit.

Gaufre: Batter cooked in a waffle-like honeycomb mold. Usually simply sprinkled with powdered sugar or topped with whipped cream (*Chantilly*) or hot fudge.

Guinette: Piece of chocolate with a maraschino cherry and kirsch-based liqueur inside.

Langue de chat: Small dry biscuit in an oblong "tongue" shape.

Macaron: Soft dome-shaped biscuit made with almond paste, egg whites and sugar.

Marron glacé: This is a candied whole chestnut, coated with a syrup glazing.

Pain d'épices: A strong, compact dark brown pound cake made with rye flour, honey and sugar.

Petit-fours: Assortment of bite-sized tarts, or little pastries filled with confectioner's custard, fruit marmelade or almond paste.

Pets-de-Nonne: Small puff balls similar to "doughnut holes" that are deep fried, then rolled in sugar.

Sarment du Médoc: Long, pretzel-thin chocolate sticks with orange, mint or coffee flavoring.

Tuiles aux amandes: These are tunnel-shaped biscuits in the shape of "roof tiles" covered with shaved almonds.

In France, cheese production is so widespread and diversified that the familiar boast that this country has more different kinds of cheeses than any country in Europe, is normally taken for granted by any Frenchman you meet. Many of these cheeses are well known outside the country, one reason being that they have the Controlled Denomination of Origin guarantee.

The cheeses presented below are a selection of the most widely known and distributed. For each cheese, you will find an indication of the region it comes from, the type of milk used in its production, its general consistency and taste, and the characteristics to look for when selecting each type. Certainly, given the great number of cheeses represented in France (more than 400), our list will not include all of them. However, and this is generally true for other categories of products as well, when visiting a particular region, do not hesitate to ask your waiter for specific suggestions of local products to try.

Abondance: Savoy. A semi-fat cheese made from cow's milk. This cheese should have a fine skin covering and its consistency, pressed and uncooked, appears compact but tender. It is available from June to end-September. Mild taste.

Beaufort: Savoy and Haute-Tarentaise. Made from cow's milk, this pressed, uncooked cheese has a very firm consistency and is light corn-yellow inside. It is available from December to May. Strong taste.

Bleu d'Auvergne: Auvergne. A blue cheese made from cow's milk, it is soft and creamy inside with marble-like bluish mold markings. Found all year around, it is pungent and slightly piquant tasting.

Bleu de Bresse: Pays de l'Ain. This is a type of blue cheese made from pasteurized cow's milk. Inside, it is soft, yielding to the touch, with crackles of blue mold. Available all year around, it has a fresh and spicy taste.

Boulette d'Avesnes: Flanders. Produced from cow's milk, this cheese is kneaded during processing and then seasoned with herbs and spices. It has a reddish crust and is quite strong smelling. You can find it from June to end-February. Pungent tasting.

Brie de Coulommiers: Ile-de-France. This cheese, from pasteurized cow's milk, is available from September to March. It should be slightly downy on the outside and mottled with red stains. Its amber interior should be creamy but compact. Fresh tasting.

Brie de Meaux: Ile-de-France. Made from cow's milk, this cheese is available from end-June to end-February. It has a creamy and soft consistency and a distinctive golden color. On the outside, it is reddish and slightly downy.

Broccio: Corsica. Produced from goat's or sheep's milk, this soft cheese is commonly used in omelettes, various pastries, or as a filling for ravioli or stuffed vegetables. Mild taste.

Cabecou: South of France. A cheese produced from goat's or sheep's milk, it should ideally be eaten from March to the beginning of November. The Cabecou d'Entraygues is smooth on the outside, slightly bluish and compact on the inside, while the Rocamadour variety has a very thin peel of a rosy-bluish hue, and its texture is softer than the other kinds.

Caillebotte: Poitou. An unsalted cheese made from cow's milk whose white interior is very tender and rich. It is available from end-June to mid-September.

Camembert: Normandy and Pays d'Auge. This is probably the most widely known French cheese. Produced from whole cow's milk, it is at its best from June to October. It should be tender to the touch around the edges as well as in the center, and its crust should appear slightly wrinkled and mottled. Distinctive, strong taste.

Cantal: Auvergne. This cheese, found all year around, is made from cow's milk and has a pressed and uncooked texture. It has a smooth, pale yellow color inside and its crust is grayish with golden highlights.

Carré de l'est: Champagne and Lorraine. Produced from cow's milk, this cheese has a white, downy crust and can be found throughout the year.

Chabichou: Poitou. A cheese produced from pasteurized cow's milk, it is available from end-June through end-October. Inside, it is compact and outside, it is covered with a reddish crust marked with gray-blue mold.

Chaource: Champagne. Cow's milk is used to produce this malleable, yielding cheese covered with a white downy crust. It has a sharp smell, but is mild tasting. Though available all around the year, it is at its best in summer.

Charolais: Burgundy. A soft-textured cheese made from goat's milk, it should nevertheless feel compact inside and have a grayish covering on the outside. The best period to try it would be end-June through end-November.

Comté: Franche-Comté. Produced from cow's milk, this pressed cooked cheese is pale yellow inside, with walnut-sized holes throughout. Its crust is smokey gray. Generally available from the beginning of September to mid-March, it has a fresh, marked taste.

Coulommiers: Ile-de-France. A cheese made from cow's milk, it is available all year around, except during a short interval from May to the beginning of June. It is covered with a rough grayish-white crust and inside, it is a light sunflower yellow, smooth and creamy. Strong tasting.

Crottin de Chavignol: Berry. Produced from goat's milk, this cheese is covered with a fluffy whitish or bluish mold. Its consistency is quite firm. It is available from April to October. Quite strong and acrid tasting, but fresh.

Ducs: Burgundy. This cheese, from pasteurized cow's milk, can be found all year around. Its crust is slightly downy and its texture should be malleable. Mild taste.

Edam français: Found in all regions. A pressed cheese produced from pasteurized cow's milk, inside it appears smooth and shiny yellow with some sparse holes. Its crust is treated with a bright red paraffin covering. Available all year.

Emmenthal français: Franche-Comté. This cheese, made from whole cow's milk, is worked until a pressed, cooked texture is obtained. Its surface is waxy, and inside it is full of large holes and appears a warm ivory color. Available all year around, it is quite sharp tasting.

Epoisses: Burgundy. Made from cow's milk, this cheese has a brown-gray crust, a soft interior and quite a pungent smell and taste. It is available from mid-June to mid-March.

Feuille de Dreux: Ile-de-France. Made from skimmed cow's milk, this cheese has a soft consistency and quite a strong smell. On the outside, it appears grayish with red stains. It may be eaten from September to mid-March. Rich tasting.

Fourme d'Ambert: Auvergne. This cheese, produced from cow's milk, should ideally be consumed from mid-June to mid-December. It has a soft, fatty consistency with rich dense bluish mold and its crust is gray and riddled with reddish pigment. Sharp, strong taste.

Gouda français: Flanders. Made from pasteurized cow's milk, this pressed cheese has a shiny, smooth golden interior and holes. Its crust is treated with a yellow paraffin covering. Available all year. Mild tasting.

Langres: Champagne. This cheese, available from June to mid-November, is produced from cow's milk and has a tender consistency and a brick-red crust. It has a very strong, distinctive smell and taste.

Livarot: Normandy. Characterized by a homogenous and creamy filling with holes and a reddish crust, this cheese is produced from cow's milk and is available from June to mid-March. Sharp and strong tasting.

Maroilles: Flanders. With a smooth, glossy mahogany-colored surface, this cheese, made from cow's milk, has a soft, unctuous, golden filling. It is available from June to March. Powerful and rich taste.

Mimolette: Flanders. This cheese, produced from cow's milk, is pressed and uncooked. It has a distinctive orange saffron interior which is compact and fatty with some sparse holes.

The crust is thin and gray. Available all year, it has quite a marked taste.

Munster: Alsace. A cheese made from cow's milk, with a soft filling, its crust is a light paprika color. Its consistency should be extremely soft. With a powerful smell and strong, rich taste, this cheese is available from end-June until November.

Neufchâtel: Normandy. This fatty cheese made from cow's milk appears a glossy yellow inside with a downy white crust spotted with red. Available from mid-March to end-November. Mild.

Olivet cendré: Orléans. A cheese produced from cow's milk, it is characteristically covered in a fine layer of ash. It should have a firm consistency yet be yielding to the touch. Available from end-June to end-February. Mild.

Pont-l'Evêque: Normandy. This is a cheese produced from cow's milk and characterized by a smooth reddish surface and a uniform, soft and creamy texture inside. Available from October to mid-March. Nutty flavor.

Port-salut: Found in all regions. This is a cheese from cow's milk, available all the year around, whose crust bears a stamp certifying that the cheese has been aged for the necessary period. It is pressed and uncooked, and its soft interior is a light yellow color.

Pouligny-Saint-Pierre: Berry. A goat's cheese with a soft and smooth texture, it has a thin and slightly bluish surface. Available from June to October.

Puant-macéré: Flanders. Cheese made from cow's milk, with an unctuous and soft-to-the-touch consistency, a reddish crust and a very strong smell and marked taste. Available from June to mid-March.

Reblochon: Savoy. This cheese, available from June to end-November, made from cow's milk, has a pressed texture and appears rich and soft to the touch. It is smooth and yellowish red on the outside. Mild.

Rollot: Picardy. Produced from cow's milk, this cheese has a smooth and shiny ocher crust and a soft consistency. It can be round or heart-shaped. Available from June through November, it has quite a sharp taste.

Roquefort: Aquitaine. This international favorite is produced from sheep's milk and is in its prime from June to December. Its moldless crust has needle-hole marks where the cheese has been pricked to encourage the formation of blue mold inside. Its consistency is soft, fatty and slightly yellow. Quite salty and strong.

Sainte-maure: Touraine. This cheese, made from goat's milk, has a very solid texture and a fine crust which can be slightly bluish when in a "patty" round shape, or if in a roll white and downy. Available from June to November.

Saint-nectaire: Auvergne. Produced from cow's milk, this cheese has a crust covered in dense yellowish and bluish mold. Its consistency, pressed and uncooked, is soft to the touch. Available from June to November. Marked taste.

Saint-paulin: A product made from pasteurized cow's milk, it is found in all regions of the country, the year round. Its crust is smooth and its ocher interior is homogenous and soft. Marked taste.

Tomme de Savoie: Savoy. Another product made from cow's milk, this cheese is characterized by its gray crust mottled with red and yellow stains. Its pressed and uncooked yellow interior is smooth and soft. Available from June to end-November. Fresh though rather sharp tasting.

Vacherin des Bauges: Savoy. The filling of this cheese, made from cow's milk, is soft and very creamy and its crust looks smooth and slightly pinkish. Good between December and mid-March. Mild tasting.

Valençay: Berry. From goat's milk, this cheese has a very dry, navy blue crust and a consistency that is soft, yet compact. It is available from May to October. Mild taste.

Vendôme bleu: Orléans. Produced from cow's milk, this cheese is available from mid-June to mid-March. Its consistency should be compact but not hard, and its crust a dark charcoal, almost-black color.

LIQUEURS

In a great wine-producing country which is also rich in fruit and aromatic herbs, an active and age-old tradition of liqueur production goes without saying. France does, in fact, produce numerous types of spirits, all quite fragrant, dry and strong, as well as liqueurs called *crèmes*, made from fruit, and extremely aromatic after-dinner liqueurs made from herbs, spices and citrus fruit rind.

In the wine regions of France, most local producers offer a free tasting of their products in their wineshop-cellars, and often even a little snack to go with them – an excellent way to select some bottles to take home!

In the following list you will find some suggested liqueurs and other alcoholic beverages which should definitely not be missed, particularly if you are visiting the region in which they are produced.

Anisette: Liqueur made from green aniseed, alcohol, water and sugar.

Armagnac: Midi-Pyrénées. A brandy produced in the Armagnac region.

Bénédictine: Liqueur made principally from herbs soaked in alcohol.

Calvados: Normandy. A very strong liqueur made from apples grown in the Calvados region.

Chartreuse: Rhône-Alpes. Aromatic liqueur produced by the convent of Grande-Chartreuse.

Chouchen: Brittany. Alcoholic drink of Celtic origin made with honey.

Cidre: Apple cider with a very low percentage of alcohol, available all over France, though originally produced in the North, particularly Normandy.

Cognac: Charentes. Brandy produced in the region of Cognac.

Crème de cassis: A very fragrant sweet liqueur with a strong blackcurrent flavor. *Crèmes* are usually prepared from red berries or sometimes citrus fruit, however there are also banana, cocoa, and many other flavored crèmes.

Fine: Natural spirit of superior quality.

Kirsch: A spirit extracted from fermented cultivated or wild cherries. Often used in pastries.

Marc de Bourgogne: Distilled from *genne*, which is the grape residue obtained after pressing, it is a very strong and highly fragrant brandy.

Mirabelle: Very strong and fragrant spirit made from large plums.

Pastis: Alcoholic drink (between 40° to 45°) made from a mixture of pure alcohol and extract of aniseed macerated for a day or two with powdered liquorice to sweeten the taste. Diluted with ice water, it is the most popular aperitif today in France.

Patxaran: Liqueur of Basque origin made from wild plums and aniseed.

Quetsche: A very strong and fragrant spirit made from Damask plums.

Ratafia: Liqueur obtained from soaking fruit, flowers and stems in alcohol or a mixture of *grappa* (spirit obtained from the distillation of grape pips) and grape must.

Williamine: Spirit made from William pears.

The dishes described in the list below originally reflected various regional gastronomic traditions. Today, however, these dishes have become so popular all over France that the only trace of their regional roots may perhaps be found solely in the name of the dish, or in some of its ingredients. You may discover that some of these specialties are better known in one region than in another, or that their preparation differs greatly from the original recipe, depending upon the region.

The dishes are listed in alphabetical order according to their French name, and whenever possible a translation has been added in parenthesis. Also, an indication has been given of when, during a meal, the dish would be served.

Alose à l'oseille (Shad and sorrel): Main dish. Baked fish with sorrel added which, it is said, has the power to dissolve the many fishbones.

Alouettes sans tête: Main dish. Beef rolls cooked in a mushroom and Madera sauce.

Ananas belle de Meaux: Dessert. Diced pineapple and strawberries first marinated in kirsch, then served inside a half pineapple shell and topped with whipped cream.

Anguille persillée (Eel with parsley): Main dish. Although eel is an oily fish, this tasty prepration makes it quite light and digestible. It is served in pieces, after having been cooked in lots of garlic and parsley.

Assiette anglaise: Hors-d'oeuvre. Plate of assorted sliced cold cut meats.

Assiette de crudités: Hors-d'oeuvre. Assortment of raw vegetables that will almost always include grated carrots.

Avocat au crabe (Avocado and crab)**:** Hors-d'oeuvre. The avocado halves are filled with a mixture of crab, rum and fresh cream.

Baba: Dessert. A bun-shaped sponge cake pastry which is soaked in rum or kirsch after baking.

Bar au beurre blanc (Bass drawn in "white butter")**:** Main dish. The fish is delicately cooked in a pot and then served with a *beurre blanc* sauce (see "Sauces").

Bavarois (Bavarian)**:** Dessert. A very fresh and light pastry filled with fruit mousse and whipped cream.

Bisque de homard (Cream of crayfish or lobster)**:** Opener. Served on special occasions, this dish consists of pieces of crayfish or lobster in a thick cream soup prepared with white wine, onions, garlic, carrots, aromatic herbs and tomato concentrate. Before serving, fresh cream is also added.

Blanquette de veau: Main dish. The term *blanquette* refers to a type of stew made with white meat. In this dish, veal is cut into chunks and simmered in a creamy sauce.

Bœuf à la mode: Main dish. Beef simmered in a pot with carrots and red wine.

Bœuf en daube (Beef stew)**:** Main dish. Chunks of beef are marinated for a few hours in red wine, oil, lemon, thyme, bay leaf and estragon and then simmered in a pot with onions and carrots.

Bouchées à la Reine: Hors-d'oeuvre. Puff pastry shells are garnished with veal sweetbread and mushrooms and then covered with a cream sauce.

Brandade de morue (Mashed dried cod): Main dish. Dried cod preserved in salt is prepared and cooked with mashed potatoes that lessen the saltiness of the fish. Just before serving, the dish is browned in the oven.

Café liégeois: Dessert. Coffee ice-cream with coffee-flavored liqueur on top and whipped cream.

Cailles aux raisins (Quail with grapes): Main dish. The quail is cooked in a pot, flambéed in Cognac, and then served on toast with green grapes that have already been cooked with the fowl.

Canard à l'orange (Duck in orange sauce): Main dish. This is a very fine dish, exquisitely flavored with orange. Roast duck is served with a delicate orange sauce, and presented in the center of a ring of sliced fresh oranges. The duck is also very often cooked with turnips and olives, or with peaches.

Cassoulet: One-dish meal. This is a very hearty dish made with haricot beans simmered with pork, mutton, duck or goose (depending on the region), and large pork sausages, garlic, shallots and tomatoes. A specialty from Toulouse.

Charlotte aux fraises (Strawberry Charlotte): Dessert. A very light mousse, made with whipped cream and strawberries, is first placed in a mold lined with ladyfinger sponge biscuits soaked in liqueur. Served chilled, it may also be prepared with other kinds of fruit or with chocolate.

Châteaubriand à la moutarde: Main dish. Chateaubriand is a round, very thick cut of beef fillet. It is fried and served with a butter and mustard spread and sprinkled with aromatic herbs.

Chocolat liégeois: Dessert. Chocolate ice-cream served with fudge and whipped cream.

Chou à la crème (Cream puffs)**:** Dessert. Large light pastry puffs filled with confectioner's custard or whipped cream.

Chou farci (Stuffed cabbage)**:** Hors-d'oeuvre. A large cabbage is stuffed with sausage meat and various types of chopped vegetables, then tied into a bundle and boiled in a broth.

Choucroute garnie à l'alsacienne: One-dish meal. Certainly Alsace's most characteristic dish, *choucroute* is made with pickled sauerkraut and various pork specialties such as pig's feet, smoked bacon, frankfurters, blood sausage, etc., as well as white-meat sausage and boiled potatoes.

Civet de lapin: Main dish. Pieces of rabbit stewed in red wine and bacon, though very often the rabbit may be replaced by hare for this dish, which gives it a stronger, "wilder" flavor.

Clafoutis: Dessert. The batter used for this pastry is mixed together with fruit, usually cherries, and then poured into a mold and baked.

Cocktail de langoustines (Dublin Bay prawn cocktail)**:** Hors-d'oeuvre. The prawns are first boiled and then served cold with a red sauce.

Coq au vin: Main dish. Stewed cockerel in a red wine sauce.

Côtes de veau fromagères (Veal cutlets with cheese)**:** Main dish. Veal cutlets are garnished with cheese and then pressed in breadcrumbs and fried.

Crêpes: Dessert. These are thin "pancakes" made with batter. Savory, they are garnished with cheese, ham, etc. Sweet, they are served sprinkled with sugar or spread with fruit, ice-cream, chocolate or liqueur and then rolled up.

Croque-monsieur: Warm starter. This very simple dish is prepared with ham and grated Emmenthal cheese (see "Cheeses") placed between two slices of sandwich bread and then grilled. Sometimes served with a Béchamel sauce (see "Sauces").

Crottin de chèvre chaud: Hors-d'oeuvre. Goat's cheese on toast is melted in the oven and then served on a leaf of lettuce.

Cuisses de grenouilles au persil et au citron (Frogs legs in parsley and lemon)**:** Main dish or hors-d'oeuvre. Frogs legs are fried and then served in a melted butter sauce with parsley and lemon.

Dinde aux marrons (Turkey with chestnuts)**:** Main dish. This is often served for the traditional Christmas meal. Before roasting, the turkey is stuffed with minced meat and chestnuts.

Ecrevisses à la nage (Crawfish stew)**:** Main dish. Shrimp cooked in a broth with white wine, carrots, shallots, onion, some butter and herbs, then served "swimming" (à la nage) in their own tasty broth that has first been reduced.

Endives au jambon gratinées (Gratin of ham and endives)**:** Main dish. Whole endives rolled up in a slice of ham and then cooked in Béchamel sauce (see "Sauces") and then baked.

Entrecôte à la moelle: Main dish. This special cut of beef rib, is fried on a high heat and then served with its marrow and a sauce Bordelaise (see "Sauces").

Epinards à la crème (Creamed spinach): Side dish. Spinach cooked with fresh cream.

Escalopes de veau bohémienne: Veal fillets prepared in white wine with bell peppers and tomatoes.

Faisan au chou (Pheasant and cabbage): Main dish. Pheasant first cooked in a pot, then quickly browned in the oven and served with green cabbage.

Filets de dorade à l'estragon: Main dish. Gilthead fish marinated in garlic, tarragon and lemon, and then grilled.

Fonds d'artichauts à la parisienne (Artichoke hearts Parisian-style): Side dish. Asparagus and fresh cream are mixed together with artichoke hearts which are then put in the oven to brown.

Fondue bourguignonne: Main dish. This is a fun dish where chunks of tender beef are plunged into a boiling pot of hot olive oil and then dipped in any one of a number of cold sauces. The idea of *fondue* is that each person should cook his own pieces of meat on a metal skewer, dipping the meat into the "common pot" of bubbling oil placed in the center of the table on a special warmer.

Fraises au Bordeaux: Dessert. Fresh strawberries soaked in a good sweet wine.

Fraisier: Dessert. Sponge cake cut into two layers and filled with strawberries and mousse. This is a very light dessert and extremely fragrant.

Frangipane: Dessert. Puff pastry cake garnished with frangipane (see "Gastronomic Terms").

Frites (French fries): Side dish. Appropriately, these deep-fried potato sticks are very popular with the French.

Galette des rois: Dessert. This large ringed brioche cake sprinkled with powdered sugar is traditionally served at Epiphany. A broadbean is hidden inside the dough, and the "king" (*rois*) is the lucky person who finds the bean in his piece of cake.

Gigot d'agneau au four: Main dish. Roast leg of lamb or mutton served with French beans.

Gratin dauphinois: Side dish. This gratin is prepared in layers of thin round slices of potato, alternated with a sauce made with fresh cream, milk and eggs. The whole dish is then browned in the oven.

Harengs marinés: Hors d'oeuvre. Herring fillets covered in a marinade of oil, carrots and onion, these are excellent eaten simply with hot boiled potatoes.

Homard à l'américaine (Lobster American-style): Hors d'oeuvre. Lobster meat simmered in a savory sauce of white wine, tomatoes and herbs.

Ile flottante: Dessert. This festive sweet is made with stiffly beaten egg white, floating in a cup of confectioner's custard and topped with caramel.

Jardinière de légumes: Side dish. Various fresh vegetables simply boiled and sprinkled with parsley and chervil.

Langue de bœuf au bouillon (Boiled tongue in broth): Hors d'oeuvre. Although tongue might not be commonly eaten in many countries, it is excellent when well-prepared. For example, as in this dish, where it is simmered in a light broth and then seasoned with a sauce vinaigrette dressing (see "Sauces"), mustard, capers and hard-boiled eggs.

Lapin en gibelotte: Main dish. Pieces of rabbit are cooked slowly in a white wine sauce with small onions, diced bacon and small potatoes.

Lapin à la moutarde (Rabbit in mustard sauce): Main dish. First basted generously with mustard, the rabbit is then baked and when cooked, doused with melted butter and flambéed in Cognac.

Magrets au poivre vert (Duck fillets with green peppercorns): Main dish. Fillets of duck are cooked in a shallow pan and then smothered in a green peppercorn sauce.

Mille-feuille: Dessert. A puffed pastry with confectioner's custard filling.

Moka: Dessert. Cake filled with coffee-flavored butter cream. Though the real moka is made with coffee, it might sometimes also be prepared with chocolate.

Mouclade: Main dish. Giant mussels first cooked with shallots, then served in a fresh cream and curry sauce.

Moules marinière: Main dish. Mussels are cooked in white wine and shallots and then served in their broth sprinkled with parsley.

Mousse de saumon: Hors-d'oeuvre. This is a type of light fish cake prepared with boiled salmon mixed with fresh cream and thick Béchamel sauce. Served cold, in slices.

Navarin d'agneau (Lamb stew): Main dish. Lamb on the bone is simmered with turnips, carrots and peas.

Navets glacés: Side dish. Turnips are cooked very slowly in butter to obtain a translucent sheen and then are sprinkled with sugar so that they caramelize.

Œufs brouillés (Scrambled eggs): Main dish. Beaten eggs are cooked in a frying pan, mixing constantly, to obtain a lumpy fluffy texture.

Œufs cocotte aux pointes d'asperges (Eggs and asparagus tips): Hors-d'œuvre. Eggs are cooked in a poacher first lined with asparagus. The yolks remain soft and the whites cook firm. They are then served covered with Mornay sauce.

Oignons farcis (Stuffed onions): Side dish. Large onions are stuffed with minced meat and aromatic herbs and then baked in the oven.

Omelette norvégienne: Dessert. This impressive dessert consists of vanilla ice-cream on a sponge cake base soaked in liqueur and an outer crust of meringue. Just before serving, the entire dish is flambéed.

Ortolans rôtis: Main dish. *Ortolans* are a species of very fine, highly-prized fowl. They are cooked on the spit enveloped in vine leaves and strips of bacon and then served on toast.

Paillassons de pommes de terre: Side dish. Grated potatoes and beaten eggs cooked in a casserole.

NATIONAL DISHES

Pamplemousse au crabe (Grapefruit with crab):
Hors-d'oeuvre. This is a salad made with pieces of grapefruit and crabmeat blended with mayonnaise.

Parfait au cognac: Dessert. A frozen mixture of whipped cream and Cognac.

Paris-Brest: Dessert. A ring-shaped puff pastry filled with praline cream and sprinkled with finely chopped roasted almonds.

Pêche Melba: Dessert. Halved peaches on vanilla ice-cream covered with raspberry topping flavored with Kirsch.

Perdrix au chou (Partridge and cabbage): Main dish. Braised pheasant cooked on a "nest" of cabbage and bacon.

Petit salé aux lentilles: Main dish. *Petit salé* is a piece of salted pork. In this dish it is simmered with lentils.

Pigeons aux petits pois (Pigeon and peas): Main dish. Pigeon is simmered in a pot with peas, diced ham and small onions.

Pintade flambée aux pommes (Flambéed guinea fowl with apples): Main dish. Roasted guinea fowl covered with fresh cream and Calvados, then flambéed, is then served with rennet dessert apples placed on a layer of croûtons.

Pithiviers des rois: Dessert. Crisp puff pastry filled with almond cream. This is the traditional cake served at Epiphany in the North of France.

Poitrine de veau farcie (Stuffed breast of veal): Hors-d'oeuvre or main dish. A flattish piece of veal that is baked with a spicy stuffing and hard-boiled eggs. It can be served hot or cold.

Porc rôti aux pommes (Roast pork with apples): Main dish. A pork roast is cooked with rennet dessert apple, the slightly acidulous flavor of the apples heightening the taste of the meat.

Pot-au-feu: Main dish. This warming winter dish is made with beef stew meat and also sometimes with a piece of veal, simmered in a broth with various vegetables such as leeks, potatoes, tomatoes, carrots and an onion pierced with cloves.

Poule au pot farcie (Stuffed chicken): Main dish. This is chicken first stuffed with a mixture of sausage meat, raw ham, stale bread, milk, garlic, eggs and aromatic herbs, and then boiled in a broth with carrots, leeks, turnips, onions and a stalk of celery.

Poulet à l'estragon (Tarragon chicken): Main dish. The chicken is seasoned with tarragon and cooked in a pot with bacon and mushrooms, and then flambéed.

Poulet Marengo (Chicken Marengo): Main dish. A French culinary classic, this dish can also be prepared with veal or rabbit. The meat is browned in a pot with shallots, then simmered in white wine, tomatoes and mushrooms.

Profiteroles au chocolat: Dessert. These are little pastry puffs filled with vanilla ice-cream or confectioner's custard that are then smothered in hot chocolate sauce.

Purée de céleri-rave: Side dish. A delicious potato purée seasoned with celery and softened with fresh cream.

Purée de pois cassés (Split-pea purée): Side dish. Split peas cooked with bacon and herbs are then creamed with a mixer.

Quiche Lorraine: Warm hors-d'oeuvre. Originally a specialty from Lorraine, this savory pie filled with a mixture of diced smoked bacon, eggs and fresh cream seasoned with nutmeg, is today very popular all over France.

Raie au beurre noir: Main dish. Ray is remarkably fine when, as in this dish, it is simply simmered in a broth and then served drawn in browned melted butter.

Religieuse: Dessert. Made of two pastry puffs, a larger one on the bottom and a smaller one on the top, both filled with confectioner's custard and then topped with fondant icing.

Ris de veau en cocotte (Veal sweetbread): Sweetbread is browned and then flambéed with rum and, at the last moment, served with fresh cream.

Riz au lait (Rice and milk): Dessert. This is a type of pudding made with rice and vanilla-flavored milk baked in the oven.

Rognons de veau à la moutarde (Veal kidneys in mustard): Main dish. The kidneys are cut in slices, browned in a pan, and then cooked in fresh cream and hot mustard.

Rôti (Roast): Main dish. Roast beef, veal or pork (though other meat may be used, in which case it will be indicated on the menu), is put in the oven and,when ready, served in fine slices and covered in its own cooking juice.

Rôti de porc à l'orange (Pork roast with oranges): Main dish. After roasting, pork roast is delicately flavored with a sauce made from oranges, bell peppers and onions.

Rôti de veau Orloff (Roast veal Orloff): Main dish. Veal roast is garnished with a preparation made with fresh cream and mushrooms.

Rôti en croûte: Main dish. Roast is wrapped in bread dough or other type of pastry, then baked, and served in slices with its crispy crust.

Rougets en papillotes (Wrapped red mullet): Main dish. The fish is cooked in aluminium foil or waxpaper with mushrooms, shallots and parsley.

Saint-Honoré: Dessert. This consists of a large pastry puff cake with a crown of small cream puffs around it and garnished in the center with both confectioner's custard and whipped cream.

Salade niçoise: Hors-d'oeuvre. This is a salad consisting of tuna, tomatoes, anchovies, chopped bell pepper, olives and hard-boiled eggs. Rice is commonly added too.

Savarin: Dessert. A ring-shaped baba cake, moistened with rum and filled with confectioner's custard.

Sorbet: Dessert. Sherbet ice-cream made with fruit pulp or fruit juice mixed with water.

Soufflé au fromage (Cheese soufflé): Hors-d'oeuvre. This is made with grated cheese and stiffly beaten egg whites folded into a thick Béchamel sauce (see "Sauces"). The dish is then put in the oven and when the soufflé rises completely, served immediately.

Soupe à l'oignon: Soup made with onions and served poured over a slice of bread garnished with grated Emmenthal cheese (see "Cheeses").

Soupe au chou (Cabbage soup): A very rich and tasty soup prepared with green cabbage, smoked bacon, ham, potatoes, turnips, carrots and onions served over slices of hard bread.

Soupe aux huîtres (Oyster soup): The shellfish, just barely cooked, are served in a vegetable broth thickened with egg and fresh cream.

Soupe de poissons (Fish soup): A very popular dish in all coastal regions, this is a fish broth whose composition can vary from region to region somewhat. However, it is always made with a variety of different fish and seafood and is spiced with garlic browned in oil and croûtons rubbed with garlic. Rouille sauce is then also added (see "Sauces").

Steak au poivre vert (Steak with green peppercorns): Main dish. This is a fillet of rumsteak served with a green peppercorn sauce.

Steak/Frite (Steak and French fries): Main dish. This is a "standard" you will find in almost every restaurant in France.

Tarte au citron (Lemon pie): Dessert. Lemon mousse filling in a shortcrust pastry pie shell.

Tarte au Roquefort (Roquefort pie): Warm hors-d'oeuvre. A filling made with eggs, fresh cream and Roquefort cheese in a shortcrust pastry pie shell.

Tarte aux oignons (Onion pie): Warm hors-d'oeuvre. This pie has a creamy filling made with onions, fresh cream and eggs in a shortcrust pastry pie shell.

Tarte Tatin: Dessert. Apples and caramel are the main ingredients of this "upside down" pie served warm. It is made by placing apples at the bottom of a pie mold on a layer of caramel and butter, then covering the apples with shortcrust pastry or puff pastry. After baking, the pie is taken out of the mold by tipping it upside down, and is served topped with fresh cream.

Terrine de foies de volaille (Casserole of poultry livers): A cold hors-d'oeuvre, this dish is prepared with chicken livers and a mixture of finely chopped white meats which have been macerated in Cognac. The entire dish is then put in a casserole and baked.

Terrine de saumon (Salmon casserole): Cold hors-d'oeuvre. A very fine dish prepared with salmon and sometimes other types of fish, mixed with eggs and fresh cream. The casserole is then put in the oven to bake and the fish cake is served cold with mayonnaise and finely chopped sorrel.

Tomates à la provençale (Tomatoes Provence-style): Side dish. Fresh tomatoes are sliced in half and then cooked in a shallow pan with chopped garlic and parsley.

Tomates farcies (Stuffed tomatoes): Warm hors-d'oeuvre. Fresh tomatoes are stuffed with sausage meat and other types of minced meat, onions and eggs. The tomatoes are then covered with breadcrumbs and baked.

Tournedos Rossini: Main dish. *Tournedos*, a very thick round piece of beef fillet, is served on toast with a slice of *foie gras* and small pieces of truffle. A fine sauce made with port wine is then poured over the dish.

Truites aux amandes (Trout with almonds): Main dish. Trout cooked in butter are then served with shaved almonds which are first browned in butter.

Certainly, to list every single specialty and all the seemingly infinite variations is not possible here. However, we do propose below a general, yet quite complete overview, of the most typical dishes that best represent regional cooking in France. The dishes are listed in alphabetical order by region, with a short introduction for each area to give you the main characteristics of its gastronomy. We have also indicated at what point during a meal each dish would be served, as well as its main ingredients.

ALSACE

The most widely consumed product in this region is pork, and thanks to its excellent quality, it is always prized and appreciated at any meal. In Strasbourg, the delicatessen sellers are masters, veritable wizards, in the art of creating an incredible selection of delicious specialties from pork. After pork, goose ranks second in popularity, as we will see, and is used to produce excellent paté and *terrines* (see "Gastronomic Terms"). In addition, the region abounds in Rhine salmon, tasty vegetables and fruit such as cherry plums, from which excellent spirits are made.

Baeckaoffa: Main dish. A stew made with pork, mutton and beef with potatoes and onions cooked in Riesling. To live up to its name, the dish should traditionally be cooked in a baker's oven.

Birewecke: Dessert. A cake made with dried fruits. It is usually only served in slivers, it is so rich and filling.

Cacou: Dessert. This is a type of *clafoutis* (see "Sweets") made with unpitted cherries.

Délice de sandre au Riesling: Main dish. Slices of fish cooked on a bed of shallots and chives covered in Riesling wine, then served with Hollandaise sauce (see "Sauces").

Flammekueche: Warm hors-d'oeuvre. A flambéed savory pie made with bread dough, double cream, onions and smoked bacon.

Kougelhopf: Dessert. A light cake made with Malaga grapes, it contains no cream.

Schiffala: Main dish. This is a smoked and salted shoulder of pork (which includes the scapula and surrounding meat), boiled and then served with a potato and small onion salad.

Truite au bleu: Main dish. Despite its name, this dish contains no cheese. "Blue" refers simply to the way in which the trout is cooked, which gives it a bluish sheen. The fish is poached and served with Hollandaise sauce. (see "Sauces").

AQUITAINE

This vast area covers, in fact, several important and diverse culinary regions. The Bordeaux region, for example, offers a wide variety of excellent specialties prepared with fish, shellfish, and meat, as well as the fruit and vegetables from its fertile surrounding farmland, and wild game from the forests to the south and east. Despite the abundance of these products and particularly wild game, the specialty in the Bordeaux area as well as all Aquitaine, however, still remains pork, with goose also very popular.
This is also true of the bordering Pyrenées region, another rich culinary territory. As for the Gascogne area, it is quite

simply referred to as "the land of milk and honey," because of its impressive gastronomy and the beautiful way its dishes are traditionally presented. This area stretches all the way to "Basque country" which also boasts a rich and varied gastronomy with a marked Spanish influence and exciting spiciness.

Arroltz ta xingar: Basque region. Main dish. Fried Bayonne raw ham and eggs.

Cannelets: Dessert. Little cakes typically found around Bordeaux, crunchy outside, soft inside. They are easily recognizable by the grooves around the outside.

Cassolette de pibales: Basque region. Hors-d'oeuvre. *Pibales* are young eels, about 1$^1/_2$ inches (3 centimeters) long, prepared with garlic and hot chili pepper.

Cèpes à la bordelaise: Side dish. The so-called "Bordeaux" boletus mushrooms are very well known and appreciated by gourmets. They are fried and then before served sprinkled with garlic and parsley.

Chipirons farcis à l'encre: Basque region. Hors-d'oeuvre or main Dish. *Chipirons* are a type of squid. In this dish they are cooked in a spicy sauce and then the squid's ink is added to the preparation.

Crème au vin de Sauternes/de Bordeaux: Dessert. This is made with egg yolks and Sauternes white wine or Bordeaux red wine blended with beaten egg whites. Served very cold.

Entrecôte à la bordelaise: Main dish. A very simple dish typical of the Bordeaux area, *entrecôte* (similar to a very thick sirloin steak) is barbecued on sarments (grapevine twigs) and when cooked, covered with chopped shallots.

Foie gras d'oie frais aux raisins: Hors-d'oeuvre. This is truly a delicacy. The *foie gras* is macerated in Cognac before being cooked with green grapes. It is then served with its juice, usually on toast.

Garbure: Béarn soup made with cabbage and goose *confit* (see "Gastronomic Terms").

Gâteau basque: Dessert. Basque region. This is confectioner's custard flavored with rum or vanilla and spread over a flaky crust.

Lamproie à la bordelaise: Main dish. Lamprey fish is first marinated in Bordeaux wine, cooked and flambéed, before being simmered in a sauce prepared with leeks, aromatic herbs and just a hint of chocolate. This gives the dish its original flavor.

Mias or millas girondin: Dessert. The top half of this cake resembles a light flan and the bottom half a thicker, more compact custard pudding. It is prepared with bitter almonds and lemon rind.

Muxuk: Basque region. Dessert. These are macaroons made with sugar, egg whites and shaved almonds, which are served with walnut pudding and cider.

Piperade: Basque region. Side dish. Mild chili peppers as well as red hot ones, bell peppers, onions, garlic and tomatoes are all simmered together. Just before serving, beaten eggs are blended into the preparation.

Poulet basquaise: Basque region. Main dish. This dish consists of chicken cooked with chili peppers and bell peppers.

Pruneaux au Sauternes: Dessert. Prunes, boiled for a few minutes in Sauternes wine with sugar and cinnamon, are then placed in the refrigerator for at least two days to macerate. Served chilled.

Riz Gaxuxa: Basque region. One-dish meal. Garlic, onions, chicken, hot chili peppers, pieces of ham, chorizo sausage and bell peppers are fried together. Rice is then added to the mixture to complete the dish.

Salade landaise: Hors-d'oeuvre. A garnishing of *gésiers confits*, *jambon de magret* and *foie gras* (see "Cold Cuts") are served on a green salad with sauce vinaigrette (see "Sauces") as dressing.

Salmis de palombes: Hors-d'oeuvre or main dish. Woodpigeons, first browned and then flambéed, are then simmered in a sauce with wine, garlic, shallots and ham.

Sauté d'agneau à la navarraise: Main dish. A lamb stew with onions and a few pinches of garlic, paprika and Cayenne chili powder, this is a quick and easy dish to prepare, that will always be appreciated for its genuine Southwest flavor.

Tourons: Dessert. These sweets can come in a variety of shapes, but they are always made with ground almonds, sugar, egg yolks and honey and sometimes with pieces of almond and pistachios added.

Tourte gasconne: Apple tart flavored with Armagnac.

Zikiro: Basque region. Main dish. Pieces of mutton cooked on the spit over a wood fire and basted during cooking with a sauce made with vinegar, chopped garlic, chili, oil, salt and water.

AUVERGNE

It is commonly believed that this region's cuisine is simply limited to pork *potées* (a type of stew) and rich soups. Although it is true that these dishes form an important part of Auvergne's culinary tradition, it is also a fact that every region of France claims to have its own *potée*! It would therefore be worthwhile to consider some of the other fine specialties of the central provinces as well, as for example, stuffed hare, trout, crawfish, or the renowned partridge with cabbage.

Pounti auvergnate: One-dish meal. A baked country dish made with minced pork, beet greens and chopped pitted prunes in a mixture of eggs, milk and flour. *Pounti* may be served hot or cold and is usually presented in its baking dish.

Tarte Ervalenta: Main dish. Stewed duck with green lentils baked in the oven in a shortcrust pastry pie shell.

Truites aux laitues: Main dish. Trout stuffed with a light fish purée and then wrapped in lettuce leaves and simmered in their juices. Served with this juice blended with Hollandaise sauce (see "Sauces").

BURGUNDY

The reputation of Burgundy's cooking rivals only that of its famous wines – superb. It is a powerful yet subtle type of cuisine made for robust eaters with big appetites. Wine is often an important ingredient in its recipes and marvelously complements the region's excellent meat and poultry (for example Charolais beef and Bresse chicken), as well as fish, not to mention its famous snails renowned the world over.

Bœuf bourguignon: Main dish. Beef rump from the excellent Charolles production is stewed in red Burgundy wine with carrots, onions, bacon, mushrooms and butter. The meat is kept simmering for at least three hours and then the dish is flambéed just before being served, piping hot.

Escargots à la bourguignonne: Warm hors-d'oeuvre. The empty snail shells are filled with the snail meat mixed with a paste of butter, garlic, shallots, parsley and lemon. They are then baked in the oven before serving.

Œufs en meurette: Warm hors-d'oeuvre. These are poached eggs served on toast and covered with a wine sauce including diced bacon, onion, shallots and butter.

Pôchouse: Main dish or hors-d'oeuvre. This is a *bouillabaisse* (see p. 54) of freshwater fish such as pike, eel, carp, tench and perch simmered in Aligoté Burgundy wine and served with croûtons rubbed with garlic. The recipe for this dish dates back to 1598.

Poire belle dijonnaise: Dessert. A whole pear is peeled and poached in a vanilla-flavored syrup and then covered with a thick raspberry sauce. It is served with blackcurrant ice-cream sprinkled with roasted almonds.

Poulet à la crème: Main dish. This is prepared by simmering pieces of chicken in white wine and onions. Just before serving, a bowl of fresh cream blended with egg yolk is mixed into the sauce.

BRITTANY

The coast of Brittany is one of the most renowned gastronomic areas of France thanks to its abundance of shellfish, served raw as well as cooked. The region is also famous for its extraordinary variety of *crêpes* which you will find, whether sweet or savory, rich or plain, always available most anywhere, and at most anytime. As for "heftier" specialties, dishes such as mutton with haricot beans or tripe in cider are typical of the region.

Crêpe bretonne: Dessert. Genuine, inimitable Breton crêpes are cooked on a special hotplate called a *crêpière*. Crêpes can come flavored with a few drops of liqueur, or served rolled up with orange marmelade filling.

Gâteau breton: Dessert. This is a specialty prepared all over the region and consists of a thick pie flavored delicately with rum.

Soupe aux huîtres: This is a soup which combines an excellent vegetable soup and fumet (see "Gastronomic Terms") which heightens the contrasting freshness of the oysters.

CENTRAL REGION

The great number of restaurants to be found in this region are generally all of very high caliber. The ones located in the

villages along rivers often offer the added attraction of a little garden where you can stop and have a quiet meal, an afternoon tea, or a small sweet or savory snack of crêpes or an assortment of the excellent local cold cut meats.
As for the region's specialties, not all gourmets agree: some insist that the veal fillets prepared in restaurants along the Loire are the best in the country, while others argue that the cockerel in wine sauce definitely has no equal in all of France. At any rate, the excellent cheeses must not be left out either, those made from goat's milk being particularly renowned.

Brochet à l'orléannaise: Main dish. This is a large baked pike served in *beurre orléanais* which is a sauce made with vinegar, shallots, egg yolks and butter.

Faux-filet à la Berrichonne: Main dish. This is a thick steak that is first fried and then covered with a wine sauce made of meat gelatine, garlic and shallots, seasoned with herbs and then blended together with fresh chicken's blood.

Glace Nelusko: Dessert. This is coffee ice-cream flavored with Cognac and served with a hot chocolate sauce topping.

Saupiquet du Morvan: Main dish. Slices of cooked ham with truffles, Madera and Béarnaise sauce (see "Sauces").

CHAMPAGNE

Cold cut meats come first place by far among the gastronomic specialties of this region. The most renowned products being *andouillette* made from Troyes mutton, or delicacies such as stuffed pork tongue and the fine Reims ham. The mutton and fish from this region are particularly renowned for their quality and are beautifully complemented by the excellent wines produced in Champagne.

Brochet à l'ardennaise: Main dish. Fillets of pike garnished with a *julienne* (see "Gastronomic Terms") of Ardenne ham, then covered with a champagne sauce thickened with cream and butter.

Côtes de porc à l'ardennaise: Main dish. Boned pork chops stuffed with puréed chanterelle girolle mushrooms, then wrapped in a bundle held with string and cooked in cream and parsley.

Poulet sauté au champagne: Main dish. Chicken is sautéed in a sauce made of champagne, fresh cream and cultivated mushrooms and makes an excellent dish to be served with champagne.

Turinos: Dessert. This is a cake filled with confectioner's custard covered with an almond paste frosting.

FRANCHE-COMTE

The Franche-Comté region, and particularly its Jura area, is widely known for its excellent beef, as well as for the milk from which superb cheeses are produced. Its rivers and streams yield a great variety of fish which the local people know just how to prepare. Cold cut meats also hold their own with, notably, the smoked ham from Luxeuil as one of the finest.

Tarte tante Catherine: Dessert. A pie shell filled with apples, pears and apricots and a caramel topping.

Truites farcies Luxeuil: Main dish. Trout stuffed with salmon *quenelle* served with melted butter, fresh herbs and lemon.

ILE-DE-FRANCE

It is often said that Paris, the symbol of Ile-de-France gastronomic tradition, does not in fact possess any specialties it can truly call its own, and that it is merely a crossroads of various regional and European cuisines. It is argued, however, that this can certainly not be true if one considers that most of the best cordons bleu chefs in France are to be found in Parisian restaurants...

Aiguillettes de saumon Turenne: Main dish. Fillets of salmon are smothered in a light fish purée. Mushrooms, cucumbers and tomatoes are then added as a finishing touch.

Médaillons de veau "Bergerette": Main dish. These are small medallion-shaped patties of marinated veal that are first sautéed, then flambéed and served in a mushroom and cream sauce with asparagus tips and small browned potatoes on the side.

Omelette soufflée flambée au rhum: Dessert. A frothy, sweet omelette that makes the perfect dessert for a light meal.

Ris de veau Joseph: Hors-d'oeuvre. Veal sweetbread cooked in fresh cream whose juices have first been deglazed with Noilly, Madeira and Cognac.

Soles au champagne: Main dish. Sole garnished with pike *quenelles* (see "Gastronomic Terms") and mushrooms, the fish is then cooked in champagne, which produces an excellent sauce.

LANGUEDOC-ROUSSILLON

If you happen to be on the coast, be sure not to miss the fresh grilled sardines, served hot on country bread right on the beach, with the excellent, freely flowing local white wine. You will also find that pork also occupies a predominant place in meals, as well as patés made with liver, turkey, duck and goose.

Loup de la méditerranée braisé au Ricard: Bass, one of the finest fish found in the Mediterranean, is stuffed with a *julienne* of herbs and vegetables, and then wrapped in lettuce leaves and braised. The juice is then blended with a Béarnaise sauce (see "Sauces") with lots of tarragon and then given a pleasant twist of aniseed flavoring thanks to some Ricard (an aniseed aperitif).

Omelette soufflée à la Verveine du Velay: Dessert. Verveine du Vélay, a liqueur produced in the region, is used to deliciously flavor this very light omelette that has the consistency of a soufflé.

Petite marmite des montagnards ariégeois: Main dish. Vegetables, meat and stuffed poultry are combined in a pot and boiled.

LIMOUSIN

This region, which includes the Corrèze and Haute-Vienne areas, despite its relatively small size, enjoys a very widespread gastronomic reputation. The popular specialty, stuffed hare, is said to have originated in this region, which also boasts a variety of rich and tasty soups (often with cabbage) and remarkable *foie gras* patés.

"Baron" d'agneau à la limousine: Main dish. Slices of roast lamb are flavored during cooking with a special aromatic oil and then served with a *garniture limousine* (see below).

Garniture limousine: Side dish. Potato and tomato, stuffed with mushrooms and whole chestnuts, provide a delicate spread for toast covered with slices of mountain ham.

LORRAINE

Meals in Lorraine generally speaking are big and hearty, like the appetites of the people of this region. Right on top of the list of specialties comes the famous *potée*, a special vegetable soup or stew that has become the veritable symbol of gastronomy in Lorraine.
Local cooking offers, however, many other dishes, all quite rich and solid, such as snails with eggs, onion pie, or the all-time favorite, *quiche*, a savory pie served in practically all restaurants and cafés in the region (in fact, *quiche* is also a standard dish in nearby Alsace, where all cooks claim to possess the original recipe).

Foie gras des Ducs de Lorraine: Main dish. For this dish, foie gras is crushed and then left in a truffle marinade. Afterwards, it is creamed until its texture is compact. The preparation is then poached and becomes a particularly smooth and tasty dish.

Quiche Lorraine: Warm hors-d'oeuvre. This is a savory pie prepared with bacon, beaten eggs and cream to which fine slices of cheese are often added. In any of its infinite variations, it is always a tasty favorite.

Truites Nano: Main dish. Trout stuffed with finely chopped sorrel, spinach, fresh mint, then baked.

MIDI-PYRÉNÉES

This region, located in the Southwest, shares many of the same culinary characteristics as its neighboring regions, Aquitaine and Languedoc-Rousillon. A great number of tasty dishes made from game, poultry, lard, lamb and pork, served along with a variety of succulent vegetables make up its repertoire, including the famous specialty, *cassoulet*.
Also the icy, torrential streams of the Pyrénées yield a great variety of fish used in other specialties. All of these dishes are accompanied by the excellent local wines. If you visit the area, do not miss trying the Quercy truffles either, or the frogs legs prepared according to a number of traditional recipes.

Cou d'oie farci (Stuffed goose neck): Hors-d'oeuvre. This delicacy is first prepared by marinating the skin from a goose neck in white wine and herbs. The goose neck is then stuffed with sausage meat, duck foie gras and truffles.

Soufflé au Roquefort: Warm hors-d'oeuvre. The same basic recipe for soufflé au fromage (see "National Dishes") is used for this dish, except that Roquefort cheese replaces Gruyère cheese.

Tournedos au poivre vert: Main dish. *Tournedos* (thick beef fillets), quickly fried, are then covered with a wine sauce made with fresh cream, tomato, Cognac and green peppercorns.

Tourte quercynnoise: Warm hors-d'oeuvre. This savory pie garnished with mushrooms and duck liver, is then smothered with a quiche filling (see "Regional Specialties" for Lorraine, above) and sprinkled with truffles. This is one of the finest regional specialties.

NORD-PAS-DE-CALAIS

Nearly half the fish consumed in France comes from this region, which explains the abundance of the freshest and tastiest fish ever found in its restaurants. Fish is usually prepared in a pleasantly simple and natural way. The North of France, with its rich soil, also produces excellent vegetables that are used to make a wide variety of soups customarily served both at lunch and dinner in restaurants and cafés. Also, in some of the better restaurants in Flanders near the Belgian border, unusual dishes such as rabbit and game cooked with cherries are waiting to be discovered.

Avocat Fermon: Hors-d'oeuvre. This original and delicious dish consists of avocado halves, served warm, filled with poached eggs and covered in a Béarnaise sauce (see "Sauces").

Darnes de turbot à la Bréval: Main dish. Fillets of flounder are placed on a layer of tomatoes and mushrooms and then baked. They are served covered with a sauce made from their juice first blended with cream and thickened with butter.

Gâteau aux noix au rhum: Dessert. This is puff pastry filled with walnut cream and rum which is then covered with rum and a sugar frosting.

Langoustines à l'aneth: Hors-d'oeuvre. Dublin Bay prawns, first sautéed and then flambéed in anisette, are then simmered in a sauce with fish fumet (see "Gastronomic Terms"), white wine, tomatoes, and fresh cream.

NORMANDY

In quaint and peaceful Normandy, crêpes and lamb dishes are the basic regional specialties. Butter and cream are used generously in many of its dishes, reflecting a thriving dairy activity. Other specialties are tripes à la mode de Caen, Mont St. Michel omelette, and the famous cheeses, Camembert and Pont-l'Evêque. Excellent cider is produced in great quantities, as well as Calvados, a strong, bracing spirit distilled from apples.

Coquilles Saint-Jacques à la normande: Hors-d'oeuvre. Mushrooms, Béchamel sauce and fresh cream are combined with the scallops, then put in the oven to be served as a gratin.

Huîtres chaudes au Calvados et à l'infusion de pommes: Hors-d'oeuvre. Oysters are simmered in a sauce made with apples first cooked in Calvados.

Tarte flambée au Calvados: Dessert. Rennet dessert apples are placed in a shortcrust pastry pie shell. The pie is flambéed with Calvados halfway through the baking and then, when completely cooked, is served warm, sprinkled with shaved almonds.

Tourte Augeronne au Livarot et au Pont-l'Evêque: Hors-d'oeuvre. The two cheeses are first creamed and combined with egg and fresh cream and a dash of nutmeg and then poured into a shortcrust pastry pie shell and baked. The dish is served hot or lukewarm.

Tripes au cidre: Main dish. This is tripe cooked in butter, shallots and onions with cider.

PICARDY

This region is probably the least known for its gastronomy, yet it produces many specialties that any gourmet would certainly relish. In addition to a wide selection of cold cut meats, you will discover many copious and tasty dishes made with leeks and potatoes (often tarts and pies), and pork, or Maroilles (a regional cheese). Picardy is a large apple producer, as all the regions in the North of France, so be sure not to miss having a *bolée* (special cup) of cider produced in Picardy.

Caghuse: Main dish. This is a thick slice of roast leg of pork, first cooked with onions, and then served seasoned with vinegar and wine.

Epaule d'agneau de pré-salé: Main dish. Pré-salé lamb (lamb that has grazed in meadows near the sea which give the meat a special salty flavor and aroma), is first roasted, and then served with a sauce prepared with its juice, onion and carrots.

Flamiche aux poireaux: Warm hors-d'oeuvre. This is a shortcrust pastry pie shell garnished with beaten eggs and leeks first simmered in butter. A very simple and tasty dish.

Poulet au Maroilles: Main dish. Pieces of stewed chicken are then served with a sauce made of cider, milk, cream and Maroilles (a regional cheese).

Soupe des Hortillons: A soup prepared with cabbage, leeks, potatoes and fresh peas, it is poured over a slice of bread, and sprinkled with chervil and sorrel.

POITOU-CHARENTES

The cuisine in this region is comprised largely of fish and shellfish, often prepared in quite original ways. For example, oysters may be served with *crépinettes* (small rectangular sausages), or else cooked in garlic. The Poitou-Charentes region is also famous for its superb beef and its excellent butter. In addition, the soil in the area is very fertile, thus yielding abundant produce such as artichokes, haricot beans, cabbage and onions used in hearty specialties such as potée and *chaudrée*.

Chaudrée des pêcheurs: This is a tasty country-style fish soup.

Glace aux noisettes: Dessert. This is hazelnut ice-cream containing pieces of candied hazelnuts. Just before serving, the ice-cream is topped with a caramel sauce.

Gratin de langoustines: Hors-d'oeuvre. Dublin Bay prawns prepared with cream and mushrooms, covered with grated Gruyère cheese and then put in the oven to brown.

Potée "au vieux port": This is an Atlantic *bouillabaisse* (see below). Broth, vegetables and various types of fish make this dish a complete meal in itself.

PROVENCE ET CÔTE D'AZUR

The cuisine in this area's restaurants is one of the most expensive in all of France. The fruit, vegetables, fish and meat proposed in restaurants are selected to be of the highest quality. The most renowned specialties are fish dishes and, generally, the style of cooking is Mediterranean.

Aïoli: One-dish meal. Boiled cod, hard-boiled eggs, potatoes and other par-boiled vegetables, are served with mayonnaise and garlic.

Artichauts violets à la Barigoule: Side dish or hors-d'oeuvre. Artichokes are first stuffed with mushrooms, anchovies and ham, then cooked in olive oil, white wine, garlic and thyme. They can be prepared in advance and then re-heated, but are just as good served cold.

Bouillabaisse: A delicious and copious fish soup served with Rouille sauce (see "Sauces") and croûtons. It is a famous specialty from Marseilles and can be considered a one-dish meal.

Bourride des pêcheurs: A fish soup garnished with vegetables and seasoned with Aïoli sauce (see "Sauces").

La caraque: Dessert. A "must" for chocolate lovers, this is a chocolate cake with a chocolate butter cream filling and chocolate frosting.

Pan-Bagnat: Large round sandwich (8 inches in diameter) filled with tomatoes, green bell pepper, onion, basil, garlic, hard-boiled eggs, anchovies and black olives. It is seasoned with olive oil, salt and pepper.

Pissaladière: A pizza-like specialty garnished with onions, anchovies and black olives.

Poires farcies des santons: Dessert. Pears poached in syrup, are filled with candied fruit first flavored with Kirsch. The pears are then placed on a layer of vanilla ice-cream and topped with a sauce made with fresh cream and fresh raspberry juice.

Ratatouille provençale: A mixture of summer vegetables, seasoned with herbs, garlic and simmered in oil. The vegetables can then be served hot or cold, as a side dish to a pork roast, or with poached eggs.

Socca: Flaky crust pastry made with chick-pea flour and olive oil, rolled out very thinly and baked smothered in oil.

RHÔNE-ALPES

The people from Lyon and its surrounding area enjoy a reputation of having the finest palates in the country. The cuisine in their restaurants is usually always of excellent quality even in the simplest of establishments. Pork is very often used in Lyon's specialties, which are found all over the Rhône-Alpes region. In fact, tasting these specialties outside the city may prove to be less expensive, though the same level of quality will be provided. Further to the East, towards Savoy, the style of cooking is simpler and often consists of one-dish meals.

Bugnes lyonnaises: Dessert. These are sweets made with fried batter that may be served hot or cold, sometimes with redcurrant jelly.

Escalope savoyarde: Main dish. This is a fillet of veal fried with morel mushrooms (*morilles*), then covered with Gruyère cheese and browned in the oven.

Gratin savoyard: This is a typical Savoy gratin, made with potatoes, milk and grated Gruyère cheese, and is excellent with lamb.

Matelote d'anguilles à la lyonnaise: Main dish. Eels cooked in both red wine and white wine, are served in their sauce, sprinkled with parsley and then garnished with croûtons.

Mont-blanc glacé: Dessert. A cup of vanilla ice-cream, rum cake, chestnut cream and whipped cream all combined.

Saucisson chaud lyonnais: Hors-d'oeuvre. A poached sausage served hot with potato salad.

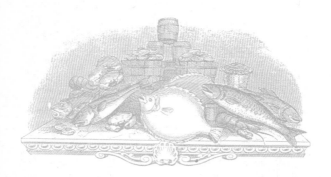

🍴 BOUCHÉES À LA REINE

Ingredients (serves 4):

4 pastry puff shells (vol-au-vents)		
Veal sweetbread	500 g	(1 lb)
Butter	30 g	(1 oz)
1 small carrot, 1 onion		
Dry white wine	½ glass	(⅛ pt)
Cultivated mushrooms	100 g	(4 oz)
1 lemon		
1 small tin quenelles de volaille	130 g	(4 ½ oz)
Thyme, bay leaf, salt, pepper		

Cream sauce:

Butter	25 g	(⅘ oz)
1 level tablespoon flour		
Juice from cooked mushrooms		
+ juice from veal sweetbread	¼ liter	(½ pt)
A pinch of nutmeg, salt, pepper		

Method:

Put the sweetbread in cold water and boil for 2 minutes. Rinse under cold water, drain and remove the fat and tissue. Dice the carrot and onion and brown in 20 g (⅔ oz) of melted butter. Then, add the sweeetbread with ½ glass of water, ½ glass of white wine, thyme, some bay leaves, salt and pepper and simmer for 20 minutes.

In the meantime, rinse the mushrooms and cut into slices. Put them in a pan with a knob of butter and a tablespoon of lemon juice, then salt and pepper. Add enough water to just barely cover the mushrooms and cook on a low fire for 8 minutes.

Prepare the cream sauce: melt 25 g (⅘ oz) butter and add a level tablespoon of flour, stirring well so that the flour blends perfectly with the butter, and a homogenous consistency is obtained. Add ¼ liter (½ pt) of juice from the cooked mushrooms and sweetbread and keep stirring until the sauce thickens. Let it simmer for another 8 minutes.

When ready, mix the sauce with the sweetbread cut into cubes, the mushrooms and *quenelles* (see p. 85) and add a pinch of nutmeg. Keep warm in a bain-marie.

10 minutes before serving, heat the pastry puffs in a medium-warm oven. Fill each shell with the sweetbread mixture. Serve immediately.

 ## CHARLOTTE AUX FRUITS

Ingredients (serves 6):
Fruit in syrup
(pinneapples, apricots, peaches, etc.) ½ can
30 ladyfinger sponge biscuits
3 tablespoons Kirsch
8-10 candied cherries (optional)
1 tablespoon icing sugar
Vanilla sugar ½ packet
1 ice cube

Method:
Cut the fruit into slices and set aside the syrup. Whip the cream with the icing sugar and shaved ice cube until firm. Add the Kirsch to the syrup which you will have kept aside. Take a charlotte mold about 16 cms (6 ½ inches) in diameter and line the bottom with waxpaper or aluminium foil cut in a circle. Arrange part of the slices of fruit at the bottom of the mold. Candied cherries may also be used at this time to decorate the base.

Now line the sides of the mold with a layer of biscuits, their

rounded, iced sides facing the side of the mold, after lightly
dipping them one by one in the syrup-Kirsch mixture. Also
arrange a layer of biscuits on the fruit at the bottom of the
mold. Then, fill the mold with alternating layers of whipped
cream, biscuits, pieces of fruit, biscuits, whipped cream,
biscuits, etc., finishing with a layer of biscuits.
Cover with a dish and a weight, and refrigerate for at least 12
hours. When ready to serve, take the charlotte out of the
mold, remove the paper lining, and decorate with a border of
whipped cream or a few walnuts.

 ## ENDIVES AU JAMBON GRATINÉES

Ingredients (serves 4):
8 endives
8 slices cooked ham
Grated Gruyère cheese   *100 g*   *(4 oz)*
1 tablespoon butter
Béchamel sauce
Salt, pepper

Method:
Clean the endives keeping them whole. Plunge them in a
large pot of salted boiling water, and let them boil until they
appear tender and transluscent (20 to 30 minutes).
Drain the endives and pass them quickly under cold water to
cool them off slightly, so that you may then squeeze each
one until all the water is expelled, being careful not to
squash them.
Roll each endive up in a slice of ham and place in a buttered
baking dish. Now take half the cheese and mix with the
Béchamel sauce and cover the endives with this mixture.
Sprinkle the remaining Gruyère cheese on top, also adding a

few knobs of butter. Let the endives brown for 15 to 30 minutes in the oven and serve hot in their baking dish.

 FLAMICHE AUX POIREAUX

Ingredients (serves 6):

Leeks	1 kg	(2 lb)
Milk	1/3 glass	
2 egg yolks		
Butter	80 g	(approx. 3 oz)
Salt, pepper		
Shortcrust pastry		

Method:
Cut off the upper green part of the leeks and remove the roots and any damaged leaves. Cut the white of the stalks vertically down the middle and wash each one very thoroughly. Melt the butter in a frying pan, add the leeks, and let them simmer until all their water has evaporated. Take them off the fire, add salt and pepper, and let them cool. Line a pie mold with half the shortcrust pastry, letting its edges fall over the sides slightly, and then put the leeks inside. Cover with the second circle of shortcrust pastry now, and lightly dampen its edges so as to join it to the edges of the pastry already in the mold. Prick the top of the pie with a fork, and at its center, open a hole about 1 cm (1/3 inch) in diameter which will serve as a "chimney."
In a bowl, beat the egg yolk with a little water. With a basting brush, brush the surface of the pie with this mixture. Bake the *flamiche* in a very hot oven for 40 minutes. Beat the other egg yolk with the milk and when ready to serve, pour this mixture "down the chimney" onto the leeks. Serve very hot.

ŒUFS COCOTTE AUX POINTES D'ASPERGES

Ingredients (serves 4):
8 eggs		
Butter	30 g	(1 oz)
1 small tin asparagus tips		
Salt, pepper		

Mornay sauce with cream:
1 heaping tablespoon flour		
Butter	30 g	(1 oz)
Milk	3 glasses	(³/₄ pt)
Grated Gruyère cheese	50 g	(2 oz)
Fresh cream	100 g	(4 oz)
Salt, pepper		
8 individual baking cups		

Method:
Drain the asparagus tips and pat them dry with absorbant paper. Butter the baking cups generously and cover the bottom of each one with asparagus tips. Break an egg over the asparagus, salt and pepper.
Place the cups thus prepared in a baking dish filled with cold water to create a bain-marie, and cook the eggs in a very high oven until the egg whites are done (8 to 10 minutes).
Sauce Mornay with cream: On a very low heat, mix the butter and flour. Add the cold milk all at once, then salt and pepper the mixture. Whisk the sauce quickly until it comes to a boil and then let it simmer for 2 minutes. Off the fire, add the grated Gruyère cheese and fresh cream to obtain a rather liquid sauce. Remove one or two eggs from their molds and put them on a warm plate. Pour some sauce over each serving and the rest in a sauce boat. Serve immediately.

RECIPES TO TRY AT HOME

 POIRE BELLE-HÉLÈNE

Ingredients (serves 4):
1 large tin of pears in syrup
Vanilla ice-cream ½ kg (1 lb)

Chocolate sauce:
Bittersweet chocolate 150 g (5 oz)
Soft butter 25 g (1 oz)

Method:
Drain the pears and keep the syrup.
To prepare the sauce, break the chocolate into pieces and
melt in a bain-marie, without stirring. When soft, add the
butter, which should be very soft as well, and 2 or 3
tablespoons of pear syrup. Mix vigorously with a whisk to
obtain a smooth, creamy texture.
Put some ice-cream in each cup, then place a pear (or two
halves) in each and top with the warm chocolate sauce.
Serve immediately.

PORC RÔTI AUX POMMES

Ingredients (serves 6):
Pork fillet roast approx. 1 ½ kg (3 lb)
Rennet dessert apples 1 kg (2 lb)
Lemon rind
Salt, pepper

Method:
Salt and pepper the roast. Pre-heat the oven to thermostat 7
(or slightly above medium temperature). Place the roast on

the rack and increase the temperature to very hot. Place a
dripping pan with 3 tablespoons of water in it under the
roast.
Let the meat brown for ½ hour at this high temperature, then
reduce the temperature to slightly below medium heat
(thermostat 4 or 5) and continue cooking for another hour,
basting the roast from time to time with spoonfuls of its own
cooking juice.
A half an hour before the meat is done, peel and core the
apples and cut into quarters. Put them in a pan with ¼ liter
of water and some lemon rind. Cook on a high fire for
20 minutes and then press the apples through a sieve or
purée them with a mixer.
Spread the applesauce in a large deep serving plate and
carve the meat, placing the pieces on top.
Serve very hot.

The secret to this dish is to grind lots of pepper over the
puréed apples right before serving.

POULET À L'ESTRAGON

Ingredients (serves 4):

1 chicken	approx. 1.2 kg	(2 ½ lb)
Smoked bacon	80 g	(approx. 3 oz)
Butter	80 g	(approx. 3 oz)
1 glass white wine (¼ pt)		
2 tablespoons Cognac		
1 bunch fresh tarragon		
4 shallots		
Mushrooms	125 g	(4 ½ oz)
Salt, pepper		

Method:

Cut the bacon into small cubes. Chop the shallots and mushrooms quite finely and cut the chicken into 8 pieces.

Put half the butter and all the bacon in a pot and warm on a low fire so that the bacon softens. Add the pieces of chicken and brown by increasing the heat. When the chicken turns a golden brown, add the chopped shallots and let them cook on a high fire for 5 minutes.

Add about 50 tarragon leaves and cover the pot, lowering the heat and letting the dish simmer for 40 minutes.

After that, uncover and pour in the Cognac, let it warm up a minute and then flambée. As soon as the flame is out, add the remaining butter and about 20 tarragon leaves. Salt, pepper, cover the pot and cook for another 1/4 hour on a low flame. Serve the pieces of chicken moistened with their juice.

 POULET BASQUAISE

Ingredients (serves 6):
1 chicken
6 very ripe tomatoes (peeled and seeded)
1 large onion
10 small green peppers
2 bell peppers (peeled and seeded)
Oil
Flour
Garlic
Bay leaf, thyme, parsley
a pinch of chili powder

Method:
Finely chop the onion and garlic. In a little oil, cook the onion, garlic, with the green peppers and bell peppers which have been cut into slices. When the onion turns a shiny white, add the tomatoes in chunks, bay leaf, thyme and parsley. Salt and pepper, and add a pinch of chili powder. Let the preparation simmer for about 25 minutes.
In the meantime, cover the pieces of chicken in flour and brown in a pan. Combine the chicken with the vegetables and cook for another ¼ hour. This dish may be served with boiled rice, boiled vegetables, or sautéed potatoes.

 QUICHE LORRAINE

Ingredients (serves 6):

Smoked bacon	125 g	(4 ½ oz)
4 eggs		
Fresh cream	100 g	(3 ½ oz)
Butter and flour for the mold		
Salt, pepper, and nutmeg		
Shortcrust pastry		

Method:
Roll out the shortcrust pastry and place it in a deep pie mold that has already been greased with butter and sprinkled with flour. Cut the smoked bacon into small cubes and place at the bottom of the pie. Beat the whole eggs in a large bowl with a fork, and add the fresh cream, continuing to beat the mixture all the time. Just salt slightly since the bacon is already salty, then pepper and add the grated nutmeg.
Pour this mixture over the cubes of bacon. Put the dish in a medium high oven for about 40 minutes. The cream should thicken and turn slightly golden. Serve hot or lukewarm.

RAIE AU BEURRE NOIR

Ingredients (serves 4):
1 ray (in one piece)	500 to 700 g	(1 to 1 ½ lb)
1 onion		
4 tablespoons vinegar		
Butter	50 g	(1 ¾ oz)
Salt, pepper, parsley		

Without removing the skin from the ray, place it in a large pan and cover with water. Add the chopped onion, half the parsley, some salt, and two spoonfuls of vinegar. Bring slowly to a boil and let simmer for about 15 to 20 minutes on a low heat. Remove the ray.
Place it on a cutting board and remove the skin and cartilage. Divide it into four parts, place the pieces in a serving dish, and sprinkle with the remaining parsley chopped finely.
Put a small saucepan with the butter on a high flame and as soon as the butter begins to brown, remove from the fire and pour it over the ray. Put 2 spoonfuls of vinegar in the saucepan already on the fire again, then pour over the fish and serve immediately. Keep in mind that any dish *au beurre noir* must be served piping hot otherwise it could be quite indigestible.

SOUFFLÉ AU FROMAGE

Ingredients (serves 4):
Grated Emmenthal cheese	200 g	(7 oz)
4 tablespoons butter		
6 eggs		

1 teacup milk or fresh cream
3 tablespons flour
Salt, pepper

Method:
In a heavy pot, on a low fire, melt the butter. Mix in the flour making sure the butter absorbs all the flour. Off the fire, add the egg yolks, grated cheese, salt and pepper. Then add the cold milk, and put back on a low fire. Let the mixture thicken, while stirring. Take off the fire.
Beat the egg whites firm. Fold them delicately into the mixture, lifting the preparation (so as not to break the egg whites). The mixture should be frothy.
Pour this mixture into a soufflé mold that has first been greased with butter. Bake at medium temperature, letting the soufflé rise for 15 minutes. Then, increase the temperature and bake for another 5 minutes until it finishes rising and turns a nice golden brown. Serve immediately.

 SOUPE A L'OIGNON

Ingredients (serves 4):
3 shallots, 3 onions

Dry white wine	½ liter	(1 pt)
Water	½ liter	(1 pt)
Butter	40 g	(1 ½ oz)
Grated Gruyère cheese	160 g	(5 ½ oz)

4 slices country bread
1 small glass Kirsch liqueur
Salt, pepper, nutmeg

Method:
Clean the onions and slice. Melt the butter in a pot on a low

flame and add the onions. Stir frequently with a wooden spoon and when golden brown, pour in the white wine and water. Cover and let simmer for 30 minutes.
Add salt, pepper and nutmeg. Transfer the soup into individual earthenware bowls with a slice of bread in each one. Sprinkle with Gruyère cheese and put in the oven for about 5 minutes to brown.
Serve very hot. Also add coarsely ground pepper and a dash of Kirsch to taste.

 ## TARTE AU ROQUEFORT

Ingredients (serves 4):

Roquefort cheese	*100 g*	*(4 oz)*
3 eggs		
3 to 4 tablespoons fresh cream		
Pepper		

Shortcrust egg pastry:

Flour	*150 g*	*(5 oz)*
Soft butter	*100 g*	*(4 oz)*
1 small egg		
¼ teaspoon salt		

Method:
Shortcrust egg pastry: Combine the flour, salt and pieces of butter by pressing and rubbing the palms of the hands together to obtain a grainy texture. Add the egg. Work the pastry quickly with the tips of the fingers and then roll into a ball. Squash the pastry with the palm of the hand, roll it into a ball again.
Repeat three times. If it seems difficult to obtain a compact texture, sprinkle with a spoonful of water, kneading the

pastry quickly. Roll out the pastry and line a pie mold that
has first been greased with butter.

Crush the Roquefort finely with a mixer. Beat the whole egg,
fresh cream and crushed Roquefort together. Pepper, but do
not salt, the Roquefort already being salty. Pour the mixture
into the pie mold and put in a hot oven (thermostat 6 or 7)
for about 30 minutes. Serve the pie as soon as it is cooked as
an hors-d'oeuvre, or cold as an appetizer with aperitifs.

 TARTE TATIN

Ingredients (serves 4):
4 tablespoons sugar		
Butter	50 g	(2 oz)
7 apples (medium-sized, firm)		
Shortcrust pastry	300 g	(11 oz)
A little fresh cream		

Method:
Sprinkle the sugar on the bottom of the mold and then
distribute some knobs of butter on top. Peel the apples,
whole.

Cut them in half and cut out the heart and seeds. Arrange
them in the mold, putting the halves back together again,
standing up and well packed together. Put the mold on a low
fire in the beginning, and when the butter has melted,
increase the fire to medium. A coating of caramel will form
and start to bubble.

Press the apples delicately with a spoon to flatten them. Be
careful that the caramel doesn't burn. After 20 minutes, this
caramelized juice will have increased in volume, and cook
the apples which will gradually turn golden and shiny. Take
off the fire and let them cool.

Roll out the pastry to a thickness of about 2 mm (¼ in). The disk should be slightly larger than the mold. Place the pastry delicately over the apples, tucking the edges in between the fruit and the mold itself.

Before your meal begins, pre-heat the oven to thermostat 7 or 8 (very hot) and place the pie on the rack at mid-position in the oven and bake for 15 minutes. Turn the pie upside down after taking it out of the oven, and keep warm so that it may be served lukewarm topped with a bit of fresh cream.

 ## TOMATES À LA PROVENÇALE

Ingredients (serves 6)
6 tomatoes (very firm)
A bit of oil
Butter   80 g   (about 3 oz)
4 cloves of garlic
2 to 3 tablespoons of breadcrumbs
Salt, pepper

Method:
Cut the tomatoes in half, salt, and turn them over on a plate to drain. Heat some oil with a knob of butter in a frying pan until quite hot. Place the tomatoes in the pan, the sliced side face down.

Let them fry on a high fire for 2 minutes on one side and then 2 minutes on the other. Salt and pepper.

Chop the parsley and garlic finely. Mix with the breadcrumbs and spread this mixture over the tomatoes. Put a knob of butter on each tomato half. Cover and let cook further on a medium heat or in a hot oven for 10 minutes. Serve with grilled meat or fish.

RECIPES TO TRY AT HOME

🍴 TOURNEDOS ROSSINI

Ingredients (serves 4):
4 tournedos (thick beef fillets)
Butter   70 g   (2 ½ oz)
4 slices of round sandwich bread
4 slices of foie gras
4 very fine slices of truffle
½ glass Port wine
Salt, pepper
Sauce:
1 veal bone
Oil and flour
1 carrot, 1 onion
Dry white wine
½ teaspoon tomato concentrate
Aromatic herbs, salt, pepper

Brown the veal bone cracked in half, in a big stew pot on a
high fire in a little oil with the carrot and onion. Sprinkle
with a level teaspoon of flour. Mix until the sauce thickens.
Add ½ a glass of white wine, and a glass of water, the tomato
concentrate, herbs, salt and pepper. Stir and bring the
mixture to a boil. Let it simmer on a very low fire, without
covering, for at least 45 minutes.
Fry the tournedos quickly in a pan on a high fire in 30 g
(about 1 oz) of butter (about 2 minutes on each side). Place
one tournedos on each piece of toast. Then, on top of each
one, put a fine slice of foie gras and a shaving of truffle. Keep
warm in a lightly heated oven. Now pour the Port wine in
the pan, on the fire. Scrape the meat residue caked on the
bottom. Add the sauce base which you will first have filtered
through a sieve. Pour a little sauce over each *tournedos* and
put the rest in a sauce boat.

TRUITE AUX AMANDES

Ingredients (serves 4):
4 trout
Milk   1 cup
Butter   40 g (about 1 ½ oz)
Flour   50 g   (2 oz)
Shaved almonds   50 g   (2 oz)
1 lemon
Salt, pepper

Method:
Empty and clean the trout and pat dry. Dip each one in the milk that has been well salted and peppered, then roll lightly in flour.
In a large pan, heat the butter and brown the fish on a medium heat for 7 or 8 minutes on each side. Watch the cooking carefully so as not to break the fish. Brown the almonds very lightly in a small pan with a knob of butter on a moderately high fire. Pour the mixture over the trout just before serving. Decorate with slices of lemon cut in half moons.

Aigre-doux: This is a sweet – and sour – sauce made with vinegar and sugar.

Aïoli: A specialty from Provence, this sauce consists of mayonnaise seasoned with garlic and olive oil, and is usually served cold.

Aurore: The base for this sauce is a cream of chicken soup which is combined with tomato, parsley, fresh cream and cultivated mushrooms.

Béarnaise: Made with shallots, tarragon, egg yolks, butter and vinegar, this sauce is best served with grilled red meat and, in particular, tournedos.

Béchamel: This is a creamy sauce made with flour, butter and milk, seasoned with a pinch of nutmeg. It is the ideal complement to eggs and vegetables, and is used in the preparation of first course gratins or other baked dishes.

Beurre d'anchois: Anchovies are combined with butter in this preparation to obtain a thick spread for toast.

Beurre blanc: This white wine sauce containing shallots and butter, is excellent with very fine fish such as pike.

Beurre Maître d'Hôtel: A sauce prepared with butter, parsley, lemon juice, salt and pepper, it is usually served with meat, vegetables and grilled or boiled fish.

Bigarade: A fragrant sauce made with oranges, butter and flour. It is particularly recommended with duck.

Blanche: A sauce made with butter, flour and water. On its own, it is rather bland and therefore makes a good base for many other more elaborate sauces.

Bordelaise: This is a red wine sauce prepared with Bordeaux wine, tomato concentrate, shallots, carrots, butter and thyme all thickened with flour. It is ideal with red meat.

Bourguignonne: Red Burgundy wine is used for this sauce seasoned with shallots, thyme, onion and carrots.

Chasseur: This sauce is made with white wine, butter, cultivated mushrooms, and shallots.

Chaude aux câpres: Butter and capers are the main ingredients of this sauce that is excellent with fish or boiled vegetables.

Diable (à la): A white wine sauce with shallots, wine vinegar, thyme, tarragon and chervil, it is particularly delicious with red meats, tongue or veal's head.

Estragon (à la): Prepared with broth, butter, bacon, onion, parsley and tarragon, this sauce is ideal with roast lamb or steamed potatoes.

Financière: Chicken broth, extract of truffle, cultivated mushrooms, aromatic herbs and both white Sauternes wine and Madera wine are the main ingredients of this sauce.

Grand veneur: This sauce is made with red wine, wine

vinegar, shallots, rabbit's blood, game marinade, thyme and bay leaves. At the last minute a spoonful of fresh cream is also added.

Gribiche: Mayonnaise with wine vinegar, pickles, capers, parsley, chervil and hard-boiled egg yolks are combined to make this sauce.

Hollandaise: This is a very subtly flavored sauce that consists of a blend of warm mayonnaise and butter and is ideal with asparagus tips, poached eggs or boiled fish.

Madère: This sauce is made with diced bacon and onions simmered at length in a meat broth with Madera wine. It is also possible to add cultivated mushrooms if desired.

Mayonnaise: A creamy fluffy sauce made with oil, egg yolks and just a thread of vinegar.

Mornay: This is a simple Béchamel sauce enhanced with pepper and cheese.

Moutarde: A sauce made with butter and hot mustard thickened with maizena, it is very good with both roasted red and white meats.

Nantua: This is a special sauce for shrimp and pike quenelles (see "Gastronomic Terms") made with Béchamel sauce, fresh cream and a pinch of nutmeg.

Périgueux: Carrots, onions, shallots, cloves, bay leaves, thyme, pepper and wine vinegar are all combined to make this sauce, which is particularly recommended with game.

Piquante: Spicy hot sauce made with vinegar, capers, and pickles combined with bacon, onions and meat broth.

Poivrade: This sauce is made with carrots, onions, shalots, cloves, bay, thyme, pepper and wine vinegar. Excellent with game.

Poulette: This sauce combines butter, flour, small onions and egg and is excellent with boiled chicken or boiled vegetables.

Ravigote: A sauce made from a base of broth, oil, vinegar and a hard-boiled egg yolk, then seasoned with chervil.

Rémoulade. A dressing for salads made with hard-boiled egg yolk, oil, vinegar, mustard, salt and pepper.

Rouille: This is a type of spicy mayonnaise-based sauce made with tomatoes, lots of garlic and Cayenne chili. It is served with fish dishes and particularly with fish soup.

Soubise: Onions browned in butter are mixed with a Béchamel sauce and before serving, the sauce is filtered through a sieve.

Suprême: It is made like a Béchamel sauce except that chicken broth replaces milk.

Tartare: A type of mayonnaise-based sauce which also has finely chopped parsley, pickles, capers, shallots and white wine added to it.

Valois: Meat gelatine is added to a Béarnaise sauce base, to obtain this sauce that is excellent with dishes such as eggs in pastry or veal sweetbread.

Verte: This sauce, made of shallots, vinegar, oil, chervil and lots of parsley, is ideal with grilled fish.

Vinaigrette: This is French dressing prepared with oil, vinegar, mustard, salt and pepper.

In France, the use of pork to create an impressive variety of products represents a rich and important part of gastronomic tradition. In some regions, in addition to *charcuterie* made of pork, many delicacies from other kinds of meat are also prepared, as for example, the famous specialty *foie gras*. Although quite a number of the products listed below are well known outside of France, there are also many less familiar ones that are certainly just as delicious.

Andouille: This is a cooked sausage usually prepared from pig's intestines.

Andouillette: Normandy. A well-known regional specialty, this is a cooked sausage usually prepared from the pig's large intestines. It may be eaten cold or grilled.

Boudin noir: This is a type of blood sausage made from pig's blood and pork suet. In some regions, onions or boletus mushrooms are added to the boudin.

Boudin blanc: This is a soft, delicate sausage made with minced white meat, usually chicken.

Cervelas: A type of very large sausage that comes in many different regional varieties.

Chipolata: This is a sausage made from minced pork meat in a sausage case made from sheep's intestines.

Chorizo: A large, semi-dry sausage originally from Spain, spiced with red chili, which gives it its distinctive fiery color.

Crépinettes: Southwest region. These are small rectangular sausages that sometimes also contain truffles and are usually eaten with oysters at Christmas time.

Foie gras: This specialty is prepared with the enlarged liver of either duck or goose that is the result of a special "forced feeding" process. Foie gras may be presented as a preserve kept in its own fat, partially cooked, or else fresh and subsequently cooked, for example, with grapes. In any form, it is considered a real delicacy. The Gers and Périgord regions are the main centers of production.

Fromage de tête: This is a jellied paté made from pig's head.

Galantine: A cooked cold cut meat made with pieces of lean meat and stuffing.

Gésiers confits: Chicken gizzards preserved in their fat, they are used to garnish certain salads, particularly *salade landaise* (see "Regional Dishes").

Graton: Chunks of pork and fat cooked together, these are usually eaten in slices and are quite spicy.

Jambon: Meat from the hog's thigh is prepared as ham, salted and then dried to be eaten uncooked (*jambon cru*). It may be tender and sweet, or dry and strong tasting. Among the raw hams, the *jambon de Bayonne* is one of the most famous. There are also other types of cooked ham (*jambon cuit*).

Jambon de magret or **magret séché:** This is fillet of duck that is dried in the same way as ham. It is usually found in slices and is used, particularly in the Southwest, in certain salads.

Merguez: A North African specialty that is very popular in France, this is a fresh sausage spiced with red chili which gives it a distinctive red color. It is made with minced beef or a mixture of beef and mutton, and is usually served grilled or fried.

Mousse de foie: A spread made mainly of chicken liver mixed together with other ingredients to obtain a creamy, compact texture. Truffles are also sometimes added.

Pâté: A preparation made of minced meat or sometimes fish, cooked in a casserole or in pastry.

Rillettes: This preparation is made by cooking pieces of pork, rabbit or chicken in fat in order to obtain a very stringy texture. Preserved in fat, *rillettes* are eaten spread on bread as a pâté.

Rillons: Small pieces of pig's breast, grilled and cooked in fat and then preserved in this same fat.

Rosette: Large raw sausage, a specialty from Lyon.

Saucisson: A large sausage with either a chunky or fine consistency, it always contains a large quantity of fat, and may be eaten raw, dried or cooked.

GASTRONOMIC TERMS

The definitions given below refer to terms you will most likely run across in French restaurants and are used to identify those dishes that more or less share certain common characteristics.

A l'américaine: Dish cooked with tomato, onion, shallots, garlic, white wine and Cognac.

A la basquaise: A term that describes any dish cooked in a mixture of tomatoes, bell peppers and raw ham.

A la braise: This is a way of cooking meat or fish over an open fire or on a barbecue.

A la crème: When this term is used to refer to savory preparations, it means that they contain a delicate sauce made with fresh cream. When it refers to pastries, it indicates the use of confectioner's custard or a whipped cream filling.

A la diable: A term used for hot and spicy dishes with a lot of pepper or chili pepper.

A l'escabèche: This indicates a way of preparing fish. They are marinated in an aromatic sauce, with the heads removed.

A la marinière: This indicates any dish cooked in white wine and seasoned with herbs.

A la nage: A term used for cooked shellfish simply served in their own juice.

A la normande: This term indicates the use of fresh cream or apples in recipes.

A la provençale: Any preparation with olive oil, garlic and parsley may be described in this way.

A point: This refers to meat cooked medium-rare, that is, when the middle still remains red and juicy.

Au gratin: This term may refer to a wide variety of dishes, but they will all either be covered with a Béchamel sauce and/or breadcrumbs (in the case of savory dishes), or with meringue (in the case of sweet preparations) and will then be placed in the oven to obtain a slight crispy browning on the top.

Au gril/grillé: This is a way of cooking meat, fish or certain vegetables. The term is often used as a synonym for the expression *grillé.*

Bellevue: This usually refers to meat or fish dishes elaborately decorated and richly garnished.

Blanquette: A white meat stew (veal, lamb, chicken, etc.) in a creamy sauce.

Bleu: A way of cooking certain fish that are plunged alive in a boiling broth.

Boulangère: This is how dishes prepared with potatoes are often called.

Braisé: Steamed in juice on a low fire.

Brandade: This usually refers to cod, and sometimes to tuna, crushed and mixed with puréed potatoes.

Chasseur: In general, this term is used for chicken and rabbit, but recipes vary. It will usually always indicate the use of a tasty sauce made with mushrooms and tomatoes.

Civet: A stew made with rabbit, hare or other game first marinated in red wine and cooked in a sauce blended with some of the animal's blood and onions.

Confit: This refers to pork, goose, duck or turkey that is first cooked, and then preserved in its fat.

Consommé: Clear broth made with red or white meat.

Coulis: Fruit pulp in a thick syrup usually used as topping for pastries or ice-cream.

Crème anglaise: A custard of a very light consistency, semi-liquid, flavored with vanilla.

Crème au beurre: A butter cream that may come in many different flavors and is used as filling for certain cakes or frosting, notably moka.

Crème Chantilly: Sweetened whipped cream.

Crème frangipane: Confectioner's custard with ground almonds, it is an ideal garnishing for pastries.

Crème pâtissière: A thick custard made with eggs, sugar, and milk usually used to garnish various types of pastries.

Crème renversée: A cream made with milk and beaten eggs, cooked in a bain-marie and garnished with caramel.

Croustade: Small garnished pastry shortcrust.

Daube: A stew made with meat or fish, simmered for several hours.

En croûte: In this type of preparation, meat, fish or other filling is encased in pastry and then baked.

En gelée: This refers to any dish served cold and covered in gelatine.

En papillottes: This is a way of cooking food, by wrapping it in aluminium paper and then baking.

Forestière: This term indicates the preparation of red or white meat, chicken, etc., that includes mushrooms as one of its ingredients.

Fricassée: Chunks of white meat or chicken stewed in a sauce.

Gibelotte: Rabbit stewed in white wine.

Grillé: See "au gril".

Julienne: Assortment of vegetables sliced in shoe-string strips.

Magret: Duck fillets.

Maison/fait maison: This generally indicates any special recipe of the house and it is therefore a good idea to ask for a description of the dish in any given restaurant. When the term refers to a wine, this means house wine served in a pitcher.

Marinade: Aromatic mixture consisting of vinegar, salt, spices, etc. in which meat and fish are macerated to give them a particular taste.

Matelote: Preparation made with pieces of fish cooked in wine with onions.

Meunière: Preparation for white-fleshed fish, cooked in butter and sprinkled with lemon.

Navarin: Mutton stew prepared with potatoes, turnips, carrots, etc.

Paupiette: This is a thin slice of meat or fillet of fish wrapped up in a bundle with stuffing inside.

Pommes Dauphine: These are made by rolling a mixture of mashed potatoes and puff pastry into small balls which are then browned in hot oil.

Potée: A dish consisting of different kinds of stewed meat and vegetables (particuarly cabbage and potatoes).

Quenelles: These rolls are made with chicken, white meat or fish, first crushed, then blended with a thick cream and flour preparation which thickens the mixture. *Quenelles* come in the shape of small poached sausages.

Râble: This refers to the part of a rabbit that extends from below the scapula to the base of the spine.

Ragoût: A dish of meat, vegetables or fish chopped into chunks and cooked in a sauce.

Saignant: This refers to meat cooked rare.

Salmis: A *ragoût* (see above) of pieces of game or chicken first roasted on a spit.

Sauté: Pieces of meat or vegetables cooked quickly in a large pan on a high fire in oil, butter or other type of fatty substance.

Terrine: Preparation of meat, fish or vegetables in a mold and served cold.

Végétarien: This refers to any dish or preparation made with vegetables and does not contain any meat, fish or cold cuts.

The first thing to decide is red or white? White wine usually goes well with fish and light foods it is true, but this is certainly not a hard and fast rule. In general, it is always a good idea to try the wines produced in the region you are visiting, as many wines do not travel well, or are produced in insufficient quantities to be exported. So, being on the spot may give you the only opportunity to try them.

Prices? They depend upon the kind and quality of wine you are looking for, and may also vary from one region to another, or from one establishment to another. French wines are known to be subject to very strict quality controls concerning origin, production, bottling, and vintage. Certain wines, such as those bottled by châteaux, are produced in limited quantities and are more expensive. One guarantee is to look for the words "Appelation d'Origine Controlée" (Controlled Denomination of Origin) on the label.

Also, things to remember that very good economical table wines are always available, and that local wines may often be a pleasant surprise.

Aloxe Corton: Burgundy. Robust white wines with a golden color and cinnamon flavor. The red wines are powerful with an aroma similar to Kirsch.

Apremont: Savoy. A slightly sour-tasting white wine as its name (*âpre*) indicates, but which is reputed to be "sour and divinely delicious."

Arbois: Jura. Fine and full-bodied red wines, dry and delicate whites. The rosé is excellent, dry and fruity, with an attractive light ruby color.

Beaujolais: This is a perfect table wine, pleasant, refreshing and easy. It should always be served slightly chilled, which is exceptional for a red wine.

Bergerac: Southwest. This region produces wines little known outside the area itself. Wines produced in the hills on the right bank of the Dordogne are finer and smoother (the Pécharmant is the most well known). Those from the hills on the left bank are harder, with more contrast. The white wines are fine and smooth, rarely dry, except for the Panisseau. The Rosette vineyard is one of the most famous, without forgetting of course the Montbazillac, which is the real pride of the region for its special Controlled Denomination of Origin certification. Bergerac also produces some rosé wines.

Bordeaux Clairet: Bordeaux. This clear, pale red wine was traditionally the only type produced in this region. The white and red wines are more recent. Clairet, not be confused with rosé, is a type appreciated by those fond of young, fresh and fruity wines.

Bourgogne Aligoté: Burgundy. A pleasant, easy, light and refreshing white wine, it is at its best during its first three years.

Bourgueil: Loire. A fresh and delicate red wine characterized by a magnificent raspberry bouquet.

Cabernet d'Anjou: Loire. Its pink color may vary in intensity depending upon the area of production, just as its taste may be more or less fruity. Nevertheless, it is generally always fine and supple.

Cahors: Southwest. This red wine, probably one of the most deeply colored French wines, is distinguished by its dark crimson almost-black color. Unfortunately, it is often consumed too young. If allowed to age, it becomes a splendid, strong-textured and well-balanced wine, with a full-bodied aroma.

Chablis: Burgundy. Light and spirited, this is the ideal white wine with shellfish.

Champagne: White sparkling wine made in the region of the same name. Pink champagne is also produced by adding a small quantity of red wine, which must also come from the Champagne region, until the desired shade is obtained.

Champigny: Loire. A dark rubyred wine, it is firm and full-bodied with a bouquet that suggests raspberries and wild strawberries.

Châteauneuf-du-Pape: Côtes du Rhône. A very special dark purple, powerful and warm wine, whose burnt aroma suggests a mixture of raspberry and iodine.

Chinon: Loire. This ruby red wine is fresh, tasty and supple, with an aroma that hints of the fragrance of violets. The Chinon region also produces the excellent Rosé de Cabernet which is dry, light and also pleasantly fragrant.

Corbières: Languedoc. White, rosé and red wines are represented in this region's production. The red wines are dark, strong-textured and full-bodied with a distinctive aroma that becomes finer with aging. The rosés are robust, yet spirited and fruity, and the white wines have a delicate taste.

Côte de Beaune: Burgundy. The red wines are smooth and pleasant. The white wines, with their delicate aroma and well-balanced texture, make them one of the finest.

Coteaux du Languedoc: Languedoc-Roussillon. The red and rosé wines from this region have earned the VDQS label (Certified Fine Wine of Limited Production).

Coteaux du Lyonnais: Burgundy. These wines are classified VDQS (Certified Fine Wine of Limited Production). The red wines are fine, aromatic and easy, and resemble Beaujolais. The rosés are fresh, fruity and smooth, and the white wines are light and refreshing.

Côtes de Bourg: Bordeaux. These may be dry, semi-dry or sweet white wines. The red wines are robust, well-balanced and make excellent table wines.

Côtes de Brouilly: Burgundy. This is one of the best Burgandy wines. It is dark-purple, full-bodied and strong, yet fruity and aromatic.

Côtes de Fronsac: Bordeaux. This rich-colored red wine, fruity and full-bodied, ages beautifully. It has remained quite reasonably priced.

Côtes de Nuits: Burgundy. Almost all production from this area consists of prestigious red wines with a distinctive firm texture, sumptuous color and rich bouquet.

Côtes-de-Provence: Provence. The excellent dry rosés are the most popular. Fruity, well-textured and aromatic, they are particularly good if only one wine is to be served throughout a Provence-style meal.

Côtes du Lubéron: The red and rosé wines resemble the Côtes du Ventoux (see below). The white wines are fruity and are best when young.

Côtes du Rhône: Rhône. These wines are of Controlled Denomination of Origin. The production consists of dry white wines, very sweet white dessert wines, light red wines,

robust red wines, rosés, sparkling wines, natural sweet wines
and wine liqueurs called *vins de paille* (see below).

Côtes-du-Roussillon: Languedoc-Roussillon. This production
includes red, white and rosé wines. The red wines are
velvety, finely textured and full-bodied, yet subtle and
aromatic. The rosés are strongly textured and quite fruity. The
white wines are a good complement to the types of fish
found in the Mediterranean.

Côtes-du-Ventoux: Rhône. The red wines are a light ruby
color and are particularly suitable as a single-wine served
throughout a meal. The fine rosés are aromatic, fruity and
spirited.

Edelzwicker: Alsace. This is a full, aromatic white wine that
is nevertheless always light and easy to drink. It is an
excellent table wine and is particularly recommended with
choucroute.

Entre-deux-Mers: Bordeaux. A dry white wine of excellent
quality, fresh and fruity with a distinctive bouquet. It is
particularly good with light hors-d'oeuvres, appetizers, fish,
and particularly with raw oysters.

Faugères: Languedoc-Roussillon. This production consists of
red and rosé wines. The red wines are dark, strong-textured
and have a pleasantly aromatic and supple lingering
aftertaste.

Fitou: Languedoc-Roussillon. A dark ruby red wine, it is
full-bodied and powerful. It is exceptional after aging for 5 or
6 years.

Frontignan: Languedoc-Roussillon. A golden-colored white wine, it is very smooth and has a distinctive taste reminiscent of honey and fresh grapes.

Gamay de Touraine: Loire. This is a red wine which, depending upon the vineyard, may be fine and aromatic, or light and fruity with a strong bouquet.

Gewürztraminer: Alsace. Excellent white wines that have a sharply distinctive, original and aromatic taste.

Graves: Bordeaux. This production consists of red and white wines. The red Graves are very aromatic, highly textured and spirited. The white wines represent a unique range from quite dry to sweet. All of these wines are highly esteemed for being fine, aromatic, powerful and spirited, yet never acidulous.

Gros Plant: Loire. A very dry white wine, almost colorless, fresh and light, it is at its best as a young wine.

Hermitage: Côtes du Rhône. Red and white wines are produced under this label. The red wines are a purple color, full-bodied and powerful. The white wines are strong textured and fine, with a golden color and a rich, aromatic and very distinctive fragrance.

Jura: This highly fertile region can be said to produce a wine for every taste: red, white or rosé wines, sparkling wines, *vins jaunes* (see below) and wine liqueurs called *vins de paille* (see below) are all represented.

La Clape: Languedoc-Roussiloon. Red and rosé wines are represented under this name. The red wines are fruity, supple and aromatic. The rosés are fine, fruity and pleasantly aromatic.

Mâcon. Burgundy. These are red, rosé and white wines. The white wines are dry, fruity and pleasant. The red and rosé wines are very easy table wines, fruity much like Beaujolais, but slightly more textured.

Mâcon-Villages. Burgundy. This denomination refers uniquely to its white wines which are smooth and fruity and excellent as aperitifs or carafe wines.

Madiran. Southwest. A powerful red wine whose rich qualities and taste develop with time.

Margaux: Bordeaux. These smooth and exceptionally delicate red wines from the Medoc region, are velvety and full-bodied without being too textured. Château Margaux is one of the great, prestigious Bordeaux wines.

Médoc: Bordeaux. The Médoc region produces red wines of noble reputation. They are very fine and richly aromatic.

Meursault: Burgundy. The white wines from Meursault, which rank among the most famous in France, are dry, but at the same time, mellow. They have a pale golden color and are famous for their smoothness.

Minervois: Languedoc-Roussillon. The red wine produced under this label is a festive bright red color and has a fine, fruity and well-balanced taste. It ages very well. The white wines are lively and warm. The rosés are fruity.

Muscadet: Loire. Dry, fine with a distinctive young, energetic and fresh taste.

Muscat: Alsace. There are many different kinds of Muscat wine, but they all have a "musky" taste and aroma in common. The Muscat from Alsace is the only dry Muscat produced in France.

Pauillac: Bordeaux. Red, strong-textured wines are produced in this region. They are sappy, mellow, and finely aromatic. The Château Lafite-Rothschild and the Château Latour are the two most prestigious vineyards in France and are therefore classified *premiers crus*.

Pelure d'oignon: This term describes a tint ranging from slightly orange to reddish brown or tawny that certain wines take on as they age.

Pinot blanc: Burgundy. This is a white wine that is closely related to Chardonnay. It is used in the production of good white Burgundies as well as in the process of making Champagne.

Pinot noir: Burgundy. A famous red-grape variety, it is used in the production of wines from the Saint-Porçain and Jura areas and also contributes to making excellent Alsatian wines.

Pomerol: Bordeaux. An impressive, full-bodied wine with a dark ruby color, it has a sappy quality and an exquisite velvety texture.

Pouilly-Fuissé: Burgundy. An excellent white wine, it is dry yet mellow, vigorous and full-bodied.

Pouilly fumé: Loire. A dry, clear white wine, with pale green highlights. It has a rather musky and spicy aroma.

Reuilly: Central region. A fruity, strong-textured dry white wine. It may sometimes be available semi-dry.

Riesling: Alsace. A dry, spirited white wine, with a delicate subtle aroma and smooth taste.

Rosé d'Anjou: Loire. This is a good table wine, well-balanced, fruity and light, sometimes slightly syrupy. It should be consumed in its first year.

Rosé de Marsannay: Burgundy. This is one of the lightest, freshest and tastiest French rosés.

Roussette de Savoie: Savoy. These are refined, yet strong and very aromatic white wines.

Saint-Amour: Burgundy. A very popular red wine, it has an attractive ruby color and a delicate, quite light aroma.

Saint-Chinian: Languedoc-Roussillon. These are red and rosé wines. The red wines are a dark ruby color, full-bodied with quite a strong texture and delicate aroma that becomes finer as the wines are aged.

Saint-Emilion: Bordeaux. This denomination groups together several different villages. These wines are full-bodied, strong-textured, warm and have an attractive dark garnet color and a truffle aroma.

Saint-Estèphe: Bordeaux. A wide range of wines most of which are full-bodied with an attractive ruby color. When young, they are usually very fruity, textured and aromatic.

Saint-Joseph: Côtes du Rhône. These are generally richly colored red wines, slightly bitter when young.

The denomination also includes a few fragrant and spirited white wines.

Saint-Julien: Bordeaux. A famous red wine, supple, fine and very fragrant.

Saint-Pourçain: Loire. The white wines are dry, limpid and luminous with a slightly greenish hue, and an apple fragrance and taste. The reds are pleasantly smooth. The fresh and fruity rosés, sometimes of a very pale color, are considered excellent.

Saint-Véran: Burgundy. A white wine with a subtle fragrance and a nutty flavor. It ages very well.

Sancerre: Central region. The most well known are the Sancerre white wines that are fine, fruity and supple. The red and rosé wines come from Pinot Noir. The rosé is certainly one of the finest Pinot wines.

Sauternes: Bordeaux. A golden wine, rich, mellow, and syrupy. Of particular note: the precious Château d'Yquem which is of world renown.

Savigny-lès-Beaune. Burgundy. Principally red wines, light, tender and fragrant, they are at their best as young wines.

Sylvaner: Alsace. A very luminous white wine, with green highlights, light and refreshing.

Tavel: Pinot Gris. Alsace. A strong, inebriating white wine, powerful yet subtle.

Tokay Pinot Gris: Alsace. Thick and strong white wine.

Touraine: Loire. Dry and syrupy white wines. The red wines are delicate and fragrant and the rosés are light and fruity. All three kinds are also produced as sparkling wines.

Vin de paille: This is a smooth and very fragrant wine liqueur, produced almost exclusively in the Jura region.

Vins de pays: A term that refers to regional wines of limited production. As they have not been mixed with other wines, they are usually of very good quality.

Vin jaune: Jura. An extremely original and rare white wine, it may only be consumed after aging six years in an oak barrel. During this period, it forms a thick grayish film, a special type of yeast, which is responsible for creating a distinctive golden-amber color in the wine. During its aging process, it will develop a captivating aroma and inebriating powerful walnut taste.

Vouvray: Loire. A vigorous, solid white wine with a golden-topaze color and an extraordinarily rich bouquet and taste which suggests a subtle mixture of acacia, fresh grapes, quince apples and almonds. There is also an excellent Vouvray sparkling wine which is delicately fruity, supple and fragrant with a fine, light froth.

A	comme	**Albert**		**N**	comme	**Nicole**
a	*kuhm*	*ahl-<u>behr</u>*		*ehn*	*kuhm*	*nee-<u>kohl</u>*
B	comme	**Bernard**		**O**	comme	**Oscar**
beh	*kuhm*	*behr-<u>nahr</u>*		*oh*	*kuhm*	*ohs-<u>kahr</u>*
C	comme	**Corinne**		**P**	comme	**Patrick**
seh	*kuhm*	*koh-<u>ree</u>-nuh*		*peh*	*kuhm*	*pah-<u>treek</u>*
D	comme	**Dominique**		**Q**	comme	**Question**
deh	*kuhm*	*doh-mee-<u>neeq</u>*		*kuh*	*kuhm*	*kays-tee-<u>ohn</u>*
E	comme	**Ernest**		**R**	comme	**Romain**
eh	*kuhm*	*ehr-<u>nehst</u>*		*ahr*	*kuhm*	*roh-<u>mayn</u>*
F	comme	**Florence**		**S**	comme	**Simone**
ehf	*kuhm*	*floh-<u>rahns</u>*		*ess*	*kuhm*	*see-<u>mohn</u>*
G	comme	**Gérard**		**T**	comme	**Thérèse**
jeh	*kuhm*	*jay-<u>rahr</u>*		*teh*	*kuhm*	*tay-<u>rehz</u>*
H	comme	**Henri**		**U**	comme	**Ursule**
ahsh	*kuhm*	*ayn-<u>ree</u>*		*oo*	*kuhm*	*oor-<u>sool</u>*
I	comme	**Isidore**		**V**	comme	**Véronique**
ee	*kuhm*	*ee-zee-<u>dohr</u>*		*veh*	*kuhm*	*vay-rohn-neek*
J	comme	**Jeanne**		**W**	comme	**William**
jee	*kuhm*	*jahn*		*doo-blah-veh kuhm*		*wee-lee-<u>ahm</u>*
K	comme	**Kléber**		**X**	comme	**Xavier**
kah	*kuhm*	*klay-<u>behr</u>*		*eex*	*kuhm*	*xzah-vee-<u>ay</u>*
L	comme	**Laurent**		**Y**	comme	**Yvonne**
ehl	*kuhm*	*loh-<u>rahn</u>*		*ee-grehk kuhm*		*ee-<u>vohn</u>*
M	comme	**Michel**		**Z**	comme	**Zoé**
ehm	*kuhm*	*mee-shehl*		*zehd*	*kuhm*	*zoh-<u>ay</u>*

I have a small child/ two children.	**J'ai un enfant en bas âge/deux enfants.** *jay ayn ahn-<u>fahn</u> ahn bahz-<u>ahj</u>/ duhz-ahn-<u>fahn</u>.*
Do you have discounts for children?	**Vous faites des réductions pour les enfants?** *voo feht day ray-dook-see-<u>ohn</u> poor layz-ahn-<u>fahn</u>?*
Do you have a child's bed?	**Vous avez un lit d'enfant?** *vooz-ah-<u>vay</u> ahn lee dahn-<u>fahn</u>?*
Do you have a child's menu?	**Vous avez un menu pour enfant?** *vooz-ah-<u>vay</u> ahn muh-<u>noo</u> poor ahn-<u>fahn</u>?*
Could you please warm up the baby's bottle?	**Vous pouvez faire chauffer le biberon du bébé, s'il vous plaît?** *voo poo-<u>vay</u> fehr shoh-<u>fay</u> luh bee-bay-<u>rohn</u> doo bay-<u>bay</u>, seel-voo-<u>play</u>?*
Where can I breastfeed/change the baby?	**Où puis-je allaiter/changer le bébé?** *oo-<u>pwee</u>-juh ah-lay-<u>tay</u>/shahn-<u>jay</u> luh bay-<u>bay</u>?*
Do you have a high chair?	**Vous avez une chaise haute?** *vooz-ah-<u>vay</u> oon <u>shehz oh</u>-tuh?*
Is there a garden where the children can play?	**Y a-t-il un jardin où les enfants peuvent jouer?** *ee-ah-<u>teel</u> ayn jahr-<u>dehn</u> oo layz-ahn-<u>fahn</u> puh-vuh joo-<u>ay</u>?*
Could you please bring me a glass of water at room temperature?	**S'il vous plaît, pouvez-vous m'apporter un verre d'eau à température normale?** *seel-voo-<u>play</u>, poo-vay-<u>voo</u> maj-por-<u>tay</u> ayn vehr <u>doh</u> ah tahm-pay-rah-toor nohr-<u>mahl</u>?*

It doesn't work.	**Cela ne fonctionne pas.** *suh-lah nuh fohn-see-ohn pah.*
It's broken.	**Il est cassé.** *eel eh kah-say.*
We're still waiting to be served.	**Nous attendons encore d'être servis.** *nooz-ah-tahn-dohn ahn-kohr deh-truh sayr-vee.*
The coffee is cold.	**Le café est froid.** *luh kahf-fay eh froo-wah.*
This meat is tough.	**Cette viande est dure.** *seh-tuh vee-aynd eh door.*
The tablecloth isn't clean.	**La nappe n'est pas propre.** *lah nah-puh neh pah proh-pruh.*
The room is noisy.	**La pièce est bruyante.** *lah pee-ehs eh broo-yahnt.*
It's too smokey here.	**Il y a trop de fumée ici.** *eel-ee-yah troh duh foo-may ee-see.*

Do you speak English?	**Vous parlez anglais?** *voo pahr-<u>lay</u> ahn-<u>glay</u>?*
I don't speak French.	**Je ne parle pas le français.** *Jeh juh pahl-<u>pah</u> frahn-<u>say</u>.*
What's your (*formal/familiar*) name?	**Comment vous appelez-vous/ t'appelles-tu?** *koh-<u>mahn</u> vooz-ah-play-<u>voo</u>/tah-pehl-<u>too</u>?*
My name is…	**Je m'appelle…** *juh mah-<u>pehl</u>…*
Do you mind if I sit here?	**Cela ne vous ennuie pas si je m'assois ici?** *suh-lah nuh vooz ahn-noo-<u>ee</u> pah see juh mahs-<u>swah</u> ee-<u>see</u>?*
Is this seat free?	**Cette place est libre?** *<u>seh</u>-tuh <u>plah</u>-suh ay <u>lee</u>-bruh?*
Where do you come from?	**D'où venez-vous?** *doo vuh-nay-<u>voo</u>?*
I come from…	**Je viens de…** *juh vee-<u>ehn</u> duh…*
I'm American/ English.	**Je suis américain/anglais.** *juh soo-eez ah-may-ree-<u>cayn</u>/ahn-<u>glay</u>.*
May I offer you a coffee/something to drink?	**Puis-je vous offrir un café/quelque chose à boire?** *<u>pwee</u>-juh vooz oh-<u>free</u>-ruh ayn kah-<u>fay</u>/ kehl-keh <u>shohz</u>-ah-boo-<u>wahr</u>?*

March 1st	**Premier mars** *pruh-mee-<u>ay</u> mahrs*
June 2nd	**Deux juin** *duh joo-<u>ayn</u>*
We'll arrive on August 29th.	**Nous arriverons le 29 août.** *<u>nooz</u> ah-ree-vuh-<u>rohn</u> luh vaynt-<u>nuf</u>-oot.*
1997	**Mille neuf cent quatre-vingt-dix-sept** *meel-nuf-sahn kah-truh-<u>vayn</u>-dee-seht*
Monday	**lundi** *luhn-<u>dee</u>*
Tuesday	**mardi** *mahr-<u>dee</u>*
Wednesday	**mercredi** *mehr-kruh-<u>dee</u>*
Thursday	**jeudi** *juh-<u>dee</u>*
Friday	**vendredi** *vahn-druh-<u>dee</u>*
Saturday	**samedi** *sahm-<u>dee</u>*
Sunday	**dimanche** *dee-<u>mahn</u>-shuh*

| January | **janvier** |
| | *jahn-vee-<u>ay</u>* |

| February | **février** |
| | *fay-vree-<u>ay</u>* |

| March | **mars** |
| | *mahrs* |

| April | **avril** |
| | *ah-vreel* |

| May | **mai** |
| | *may* |

| June | **juin** |
| | *joo-ayn* |

| July | **juillet** |
| | *joo-ee-yuh-<u>ay</u>* |

| August | **août** |
| | *oot* |

| September | **septembre** |
| | *seh-<u>tahm</u>-bruh* |

| October | **octobre** |
| | *ok-<u>toh</u>-bruh* |

| November | **novembre** |
| | *noh-vahm-bruh* |

| December | **décembre** |
| | *day-<u>sahm</u>-bruh* |

Excuse me, where's the station?	**Excusez-moi; où est la gare?** *ehs-koo-<u>zay</u>-moo-<u>wah</u> oo eh lah gahr?*
To get to the airport, please?	**Pour aller à l'aéroport, s'il vous plaît?** *poor ah-lay ah lah ay-roh-pohr seel-voo-play?*
Could you tell me the way to get to the station?	**Vous pouvez m'indiquer la route pour aller à la gare?** *voo poo-<u>vay</u> mehn-dee-<u>kay</u> lah <u>roo</u>-tuh poor lah gahr?*
Is this the right way to the cathedral?	**C'est bien la direction de la cathédrale?** *say bee-<u>ehn</u> lah dee-rehk-see-<u>ohn</u> duh luh kah-tay-<u>drah</u>-luh?*
I'm looking for the tourist bureau	**Je cherche le syndicat d'initiatives.** *juh <u>shayr</u>-shuh luh sehn-dee-<u>kah</u> deen-ee-see-ah-<u>teev</u>*
What street should I take to get to...?	**Quelle route dois-je prendre pour...?** *kehl <u>root</u> doo-<u>wah</u>-juh <u>prahn</u>-druh poor...*
How long does it take to get there?	**Combien de temps faut-il pour y arriver?** *kohm-bee-<u>ehn</u> duh tahn foh-<u>teel</u> poor ee ah-ree-<u>vay</u>?*
Excuse me, do you know where the restaurant... is?	**Excusez-moi, savez-vous où est le restaurant...?** *ehs-koo-<u>zay</u>-moo-<u>wah</u> sah-vay-<u>voo</u> oo eh luh rehs-toh-<u>rahn</u>...?*
Which way do I go to get to the highway?	**Par où dois-je passer pour rejoindre l'autoroute?** *pahr oo doo-<u>wahj</u> pah-<u>say</u> poor ruh-joo-<u>ayn</u>-druh loh-toh-<u>roo</u>-tuh?*

Things to remember

> You will easily find a wide selection of alcoholic and
> non-alcoholic drinks available in cafés. Generally, there
> is no cover charge if you choose to sit at a table, though
> prices will probably be higher for a table on the terrace.

A coffee/a coffee
with milk, please.
Un café/un café au lait, s'il vous plaît.
*ayn kah-fay/ayn kah-fay oh lay,
seel-voo-play.*

A draught beer
Une bière pression
oon bee-ehr pray-see-ohn

A lager/brown beer
Une bière blonde/brune
oon bee-ehr blohnd/broon

Two cups of tea
with milk
Deux tasses de thé au lait
duh tahs duh tay-oh-lay

A glass of mineral
water
Un verre d'eau minérale
ayn vehr doh mee-nay-rahl

With ice, please.
Avec des glaçons, s'il vous plaît.
ah-vehk day glahs-sohn, seel-voo-play.

Another coffee,
please.
Un autre café, s'il vous plaît.
ayn oh-truh kah-fay, seel-voo-play.

The bill, please.
L'addition, s'il vous plaît.
lah-dee-see-ohn, seel-voo-play.

Good evening, we'd like a table for two.	**Bonsoir, nous voudrions une table pour deux.** *bohn-soo-warh, noo-voo-dree-ohn oon tah-bluh poor duh.*
We'd like a table in a quiet corner.	**Vous voudrions une table dans un coin tranquille.** *noo voo-dree-ohn oon tah-bluh dahnz-ayn coo-ayn trahn-keel.*
We reserved a table for two in the name of…	**Nous avons réservé une table pour deux au nom de…** *nooz-ah-vohn ray-zehr-vay oon tah-bluh poor duh, oh nohm duh…*
Can we eat outside?	**On peut manger dehors?** *ohn puh mahn-jay duh-ohr?*
We'd like a table far from/close to the window.	**Nous voudrions une table loin/près de la table.** *noo voo-dree-ohn oon tah-bluh loo-ayn/preh duh lah fuh-neh-truh.*
Is there an entrance for the handicapped?	**Y a-t-il une entrée pour les handicapés?** *ee-ah-teel oon ahn-try poor lay ahn-dee-kah-pay?*
We're really in a hurry.	**Nous sommes assez pressés.** *noo-sahm au-say preh-say.*
Do you have a fixed-price menu?	**Vous avez un menu à prix fixe?** *vooz-ah-vay ayn muh-noo ah pree feeks?*

May I have the wine list please?	**Peut-on avoir la carte des vins?** *puht-ohn ahv-wahr lah kahrt day vayn?*
We'd like an aperitif.	**Nous voudrions un apéritif.** *noo voo-dree-ohn ayn ah-peh-ree-teef.*
What wine would you suggest with this dish?	**Quel vin nous conseillez-vous avec ce plat?** *kehl vayn noo kohn-say-ee-yay voo ah-vehk suh plah?*
Could you suggest a good white/red/ rosé wine?	**Vous pouvez nous conseiller un bon vin blanc/rouge/rosé?** *voo poo-vay noo kohn-say-ee-yay ayn bohn vayn blahn/rooj/roh-say?*
Could you bring us the house wine, please?	**Vous pouvez nous apporter le vin de la maison, s'il vous plaît?** *voo poo-vay nooz-ah-porh-tay luh vayn duh lah may-zohn, seel-voo-play?*
A half-bottle of…	**Une demi-bouteille de…** *oon duh-mee boo-tay-yuh duh…*
A bottle of natural/fizzy mineral water, please	**S'il vous plaît, une bouteille d'eau minérale naturelle/gazeuse.** *seel-voo-play, oon boo-tay-yuh doh mee-nay-rahl nah-too-rahl/gahzehz.*
We'd like some tap/ cold water.	**Nous voudrions de l'eau du robinet/ fraîche.** *noo voo-dree-ohn duh loh duh roh-bee-nay/freh-shuh.*

Could you please bring us another bottle of water/wine? **S'il vous plaît, vous pouvez nous apporter une autre bouteille d'eau/ de vin?**
seel-voo-play, voo-poo-vay nooz-ah-pohr-tay oon oh-truh boo-tay-yuh doh/duh vayn?

What are the typical local wines/liqueurs? **Quels sont les vins/liqueurs typiques du coin?**
kehl sohn lay vayn/lay lee-kehr tee-peek doo koo-ayn?

What do you have in the way of after dinner drinks/ liqueurs? **Qu'est-ce que vous avez comme digestif/liqueur?**
kehs-kuh vooz-ah-vay kohm dee-jehs-teef/lee-kehr?

This wine is warm. **Ce vin est tiède.**
suh vayn eh tee-eh-duh.

I'd like something dry/sweet/sparkling. **Je voudrais quelque chose de sec/ doux/pétillant.**
juh voo-dray kehl-kuh shohz duh sehk/doo/pay-tee-yahn

Things to remember

> Traditional-style restaurants are not the only places to have a meal. There are also many other types of restaurants such as brasseries, saladeries, bistrots and auberges…

Is there a good restaurant nearby?
Y a-t-il un bon restaurant par ici?
ee-ah-teel ahn bohn reh-stoh-rahn pahr-ee-see?

It there an inexpensive restaurant nearby?
Y a-t-il y a un restaurant pas cher près d'ici?
ee ah-teel ayn rehs-toh-rahn pah shayr pray dee-see?

Could you give me the name of a restaurant that serves typical cuisine?
Vous pouvez m'indiquer un restaurant qui fait de la cuisine typique?
voo poo-vay mayn-dee-kay ayn rehs-toh-rahn kee fay duh lah koo-ee-zeen tee-peek?

How do we get there?
Comment y arrive-t-on?
kohm-mahn ee ah-reev-tohn?

Excuse me, could you tell me where the restaurant… is?
Excusez-moi, pouvez-vous me dire où est le restaurant…?
ehs-koo-say-mwah, poo-vay-voo muh deer oo eh luh rehs-toh-rahn…?

What's the best restaurant in town?
Quel est le meilleur restaurant de la ville?
kehl-ay luh mee-yee-ehr rehs-toh-rahn duh lah veel?

We'd like to have lunch in a rather inexpensive restaurant.
Nous voudrions déjeuner dans un restaurant plutôt économique.
noo voo-dree-ohn day-juh-nay dahnz-ahn rehs-toh-rahn ploo-toh ehk-koh-noh-meek.

Do you have a
telephone?

Vous avez un téléphone?
vooz-ah-<u>vay</u> ayn tay-lay-<u>fohn</u>?

May I have
an ashtray?

Je peux avoir un cendrier?
juh puh ahv-<u>wahr</u> ayn sahn-dree-<u>ay</u>?

Could you bring
me another glass/
another plate?

**Vous pouvez m'apporter un autre
verre/une autre assiette?**
*voo poo-<u>vay</u> mah-pohr-<u>tay</u> ayn oh-truh
vayr/ayn <u>oh</u>-truh ah-see-eht?*

Please, could you
change my fork/
my knife/my spoon?

**S'il vous plaît, vous pouvez changer ma
fourchette/mon couteau/ma cuillère?**
*seel voo-<u>play</u>, voo-poo-vay shahn-<u>jay</u>
mah foor-<u>sheht</u>/mohn koo-<u>toh</u>/mah
koo-ee-<u>yehr</u>?*

Is it possible to put
up/put down
the heating?

**Est-il possible de baisser/monter le
chauffage?**
*ay-teel poh-<u>see</u>-bluh duh bay-<u>say</u>/
mohn-<u>tay</u> luh shoh-<u>faj</u>*

May we open/
close the window?

On peut ouvrir/fermer la fenêtre?
*ohn puh oo-v<u>reer</u>/fehr-<u>may</u> lah
feh-<u>neh</u>-truh?*

I've spilled
something on myself,
do you have any
talcum powder?

Je me suis taché, vous avez du talc?
*juh muh soo-<u>ee</u> tah-<u>shay</u>, ah-vay-<u>voo</u>
duh <u>tahlk</u>?*

What time do
you close?

A quelle heure fermez-vous?
ah kehl <u>ehr</u>-ruh fehr-may-<u>voo</u>?

May I have a menu? **On peut avoir le menu?**
ohn puht ah-voo-wahr luh muh-nu?

Do you have a
vegetarian menu? **Vous avez un menu végétarien?**
vooz-ah-vay ayn muh-noo vay-jay-tah-ree-ehn?

What's the house
specialty? **Quelle est la spécialité de la maison?**
kehl ay luh spay-see-ah-lee-tay duh lah may-zohn?

What's the dish of
the day? **Quel est le plat du jour?**
kehl-ay luh plah doo joor?

What would
you suggest? **Que nous conseillez-vous?**
kuh noo kohn-say-yay-voo?

Is it hot (spicy)? **C'est piquant?**
say pee-kahn?

I'm allergic
to bell peppers. **Je suis allergique aux poivrons.**
juh soo-ee ah-lehr-jeek oh poo-wah-vrohn.

Does this dish have
garlic/pepper in it? **Ce plat contient-il de l'ail/du poivre?**
suh plah kohn-tee-ehn-teel duh lay-yah/doo poo-wah-vruh?

Do you have...? **Vous avez...?**
vooz-ah-vay...?

I'd like/We'd like... **Je voudrais/nous voudrions...**
juh voo-dreh/noo voo-dree-ohn...

Could you bring
me/us... **Vous pouvez m'apporter/nous apporter...**
voo poo-vay mah-pohr-tay/nooz-ah-pohr-tay...

I'd like a portion/ a half portion of…	**Je voudrais une portion/une demi- portion de…** *juh voo-dray oon pohr-see-ohn/oon duh-mee pohr-see-ohn duh…*
I'd like to taste…	**Je voudrais goûter…** *juh voo-dray goo-tay…*
Could you please bring us some bread?	**Vous pouvez nous apporter du pain, s'il vous plaît?** *voo poo-vay nooz-ah-pohr-tay duh payn seel-voo-play?*
What are some typical local dishes?	**Quels sont les plats typiques du coin?** *kehl sohn leh plah tee-pee-kuh doo coo-ayn?*
What is the typical local cheese?	**Quel est le fromage typique du coin?** *kehl eh luh froh-maj tee-pee-kuh doo coo-ayn?*
What desserts/fruit do you have?	**Qu'est-ce que vous avez comme dessert/fruits?** *kehs-kuh vooz-ah-vay kohm day-sehr/froo-ee?*
We'd like a portion of…with two plates.	**Nous voudrions une portion de… avec deux assiettes.** *noo-voo-dree-ohn oon pohr-see-ohn duh… ah-vehk duhz-ah-see-yeht-tuh.*
Could you bring us some salt/pepper?	**Vous pouvez m'apporter le sel/poivre?** *voo-poo-vay mah-pohr-tay luh sehl/ luh poo-wah-vruh?*

This isn't what I ordered. What I ordered was…	**Ce n'est pas ce que j'ai commandé. J'avais commandé…** *suh nay <u>pah</u> suh keh jay koh-mahn <u>day</u>.* *jah-<u>vay</u> koh-mahn-<u>day</u>…*
May I have something else?	**Puis-je avoir autre chose?** *poo-<u>ee</u>-juh ah-voo-<u>wahr</u> <u>oh</u>-truh shohz?*
The meat is too well done/not well done enough/tough.	**La viande est trop cuite/pas assez cuite/dure.** *lah vee-<u>ahnd</u> eh troh koo-<u>weet</u>/pahz ah-<u>say</u> koo-<u>weet</u>/<u>door</u>-ruh.*
It's too sweet/ bitter/salty.	**C'est trop sucré/amer/salé.** *say troh soo-<u>kray</u>/ah-<u>mehr</u>/sah-<u>lay</u>*
Could you call the head waiter?	**Voulez-vous appeler le maître d'hôtel?** *voo-lay-<u>voo</u> ah-puh-<u>lay</u> luh <u>meh</u>-truh doh-<u>tehl</u>?*
Four coffees, please.	**Quatre cafés, s'il vous plaît.** *<u>kaht</u>-truh kah-<u>fay</u>, seel-voo-<u>play</u>.*
May I have the bill please?	**Puis-je avoir l'addition, s'il vous plaît?** *poo-<u>ee</u>-juh ahv-<u>wahr</u> lah-dee-see-<u>ohn</u> seel-voo-<u>play</u>?*

CARTE DU JOUR

Hello, we'd like to reserve a table for four.

Bonjour, nous voudrions réserver une table pour quatre.
bohn-joor, noo voo-dree-ohn ray-zehr-vay oon tah-bluh poor kah-truh.

I would like to reserve a table for two for this evening/ tomorrow evening at 8:00 P.M. in the name of...

Je voudrais réserver une table pour deux personnes, pour ce soir demain soir à huit heures, au nom de...
juh voo-dray ray-zehr-vay oon tah-bluh poor duh payr-sohn poor suh soo-ahr ah oo-eet ehr-ruh, oh nohm duh...

What day are you closed?

Quel est le jour de fermeture hebdomadaire?
kehl-ay luh joor duh fehr-muh-turh ehb-doh-mah-dehr?

What time does the restaurant open/ close?

A quelle heure ouvre/ferme le restaurant?
ah kehl ehr-ruh oov-ruh/fehr-muh luh rehs-toh-rahn?

I would like to cancel a reservation I made for this evening for two, in the name of...

Je voudrais annuler une réservation que j'avais faite pour ce soir pour deux personnes, au nom de...
juh voo-dray ah-noo-lay ray-zehr-vah-see-ohn kuh jah-vay feht poor suh soo-wahr, poor duh payr-sohn, oh nohm duh...

Is it necessary to book?

Est-il nécessaire de réserver?
ay-teel nay-say-sehr duh ray-zehr-vay?

Is there a doctor here?	**Y a-t-il un docteur ici?** *ee-ah-<u>teel</u> ayn dohk-<u>tehr</u> ee-<u>see</u>?*
Call a doctor/ an ambulance!	**Appelez un docteur/une ambulance!** *ah-<u>play</u> ayn dohk-<u>tehr</u>/oon ahm-boo-<u>lahns</u>!*
Get help, quick!	**Allez chercher de l'aide, vite!** *ah-<u>lay</u> shehr-shay dul-<u>lehd</u>, veet!*
My wife is in labor.	**Ma femme est sur le point d'accoucher.** *mah <u>fahm</u>-muh ay soor luh poo-<u>ayn</u> dah-koo-<u>shay</u>.*
Where is the nearest police station/ hospital?	**Où est le poste de police/l'hôpital le plus proche?** *oo ay luh <u>pohst</u> duh poh-<u>lees</u>/loh-pee-<u>tahl</u> luh ploo <u>proh</u>-shuh?*
I've lost my credit card/my wallet.	**J'ai perdu ma carte de crédit/mon portefeuille.** *jay pehr-<u>doo</u> mah kahrt duh <u>kray</u>-dee/mohn pohr-toh-<u>feh</u>-ee-yuh*
I've lost my child/ my handbag	**J'ai perdu mon enfant/mon sac.** *jay pehr-<u>doo</u> mohn ahn-<u>fahn</u>/mohn sahk.*

Are there any nightclubs?	**Est-ce qu'il y a des boîtes de nuit?** *ehs-keel-ee-ah day boo-aht duh noo-ee?*
Are there any special places/ shows for children?	**Y a-t-il des endroits/des spectacles réservés aux enfants?** *ee-ah-teel dayz-ahn-drwah/day spay-tah-kluh ray-zehr-vay ohz ahn-fahn?*
What's there to do at night?	**Qu'est-ce qu'il y a à faire le soir?** *kehs-keel-ee-ah ah fehr luh swahr?*
Where's there a cinema/a theater?	**Où y a-t-il un cinéma/un théâtre?** *oo-ee-ah-teel ayn see-nay-mah/ayn tay-ah-truh?*
Could you book some tickets for us?	**Vous pouvez nous réserver des billets?** *voo poo-vay noo ray-zehr-vay day bee-yay?*
Is there a swimming pool?	**Est-ce qu'il y a une piscine?** *ehs-keel-ee-ah oon pee-seen?*
Are there any nice day trips to take?	**Est-ce qu'il y a de belles excursions à faire?** *ehs-keel-ee-ah duh behlz ehs-kehr-see-ohn ah fayr?*
Where can we play tennis/golf?	**Où peut-on jouer au tennis/au golf?** *oo puht-ohn joo-way ph tehn-nees/oh gohl-fuh?*
Is it possible to go horseback riding/ to fish?	**Est-ce qu'il est possible de monter à cheval/pêcher?** *ay-teel poh-see-bluh duh mohn-tay ah shuh-vahl/duh pay-shay?*

EXPRESSIONS 1

Hello (during the day) Good morning/ afternoon	**Bonjour** *bohn-joor*
Hello (in the evening) Good evening	**Bonsoir** *bohn-soo-wahr*
Good night	**Bonne nuit** *behn-noo-ee*
Good-bye	**Au revoir** *oh-reh-voo-wahr*
See you soon!	**A bientôt!** *ah been-ehn-toh*
My pleasure!	**Très heureux!** *trehz-ehr-ruh*
How are you?	**Comment allez-vous?** *kohm-mahn-tah-lay voo?*
Very well, thank you.	**Bien, merci.** *bee-ehn, mehr-see*
Please	**S'il vous plaît** *seel-voo-play*

Excuse me (sorry…)	**Excusez-moi** *ehk-skoo-<u>zay</u> moo-<u>wah</u>*
I'm sorry.	**Je suis désolé.** *juh soo-ee day-zoh-lay*
Thank you (very much).	**Merci (beaucoup).** *mehr-<u>see</u> (boh-<u>koo</u>)*
Yes/no thank you	**Oui/non merci** *oo-<u>ee</u>/nohn mehr-<u>see</u>*
I/we would like…	**Je voudrais/nous voudrions…** *juh voo-<u>dray</u>/noo voo-dree-<u>ohn</u>*

Things to remember

> For cold cut meats and cheeses, by far the best places to shop are the charcuteries, which always carry a wide selection of quality products. As for other purchases (wine, liqueurs, pasta, oil, etc.) supermarkets have quality products at reasonable prices.

Is this a fresh cheese?	**C'est un fromage frais?** *say-tayn froh-mahj freh?*
Is this a sweet wine?	**C'est un vin doux?** *say-tayn vayn doo?*
How much is it a kilo/100 grams?	**Combien coûte le kilo/les 100 grammes?** *kohm-bee-ehn koot luh kee-loh? lay sahn grahm?*
How long does it keep?	**Combien de temps se conserve-t-il?** *kohm-bee-ehn duh tahn suh kohn-sehr-vuh-teel?*
I'll take this one/ that one.	**Je prends celui-ci/celui-là** *Juh prahn suh-loo-ee-see/ suh-loo-ee-lah*
I would like two bottles.	**J'en voudrais deux bouteilles.** *jahn voo-dray duh boo-teh-yuh.*
Give me half a kilo.	**Donnez-m'en un demi-kilo.** *dohn-nay-mahn ayn duh-mee kee-loh.*
Could you wrap it up for traveling?	**Vous pouvez me l'emballer pour le voyage?** *voo poo-vay muh-lam-bah-lay poor luh voh-ee-yaj?*

ARTICLES

Words for "the": (le/la/les) (the)
luh/lah/lay

Masculine singular *Feminine singular*
le **la**
l' (before a vowel) **l'** (before a vowel)

Masculine plural *Feminine plural*
les **les**

Words for "a" or "an":
(un/une) (a or an)
ayn/oon

Masculine *Feminine*
un **une**

When articles are preceded by the prepositions **à** (to or at) or **de** (of/from) the following contractions are used:

à+le = au *oh* **de+le = du** *doo*
à+les = aux *oh* **de+les = des** *deh*

Ex: **au cinéma** (to or at the cinema)
oh see-nay-mah
le prix du billet (the price of the ticket)
luh pree doo bee-yay

NOUNS

Plurals

In most cases, the plural is formed by adding **-s** (though it is silent) to the end of the word:

Masculine singular
le livre (the book)
luh <u>leev</u>-ruh

Feminine singular
la pomme (the apple)
lah <u>puhm</u>-muh

Masculine plural
les livres (the books)
lay <u>leev</u>-ruh

Masculine plural
les pommes (the apples)
lay <u>puhm</u>-muh

ADJECTIVES

Adjectives in French, unlike English, agree in gender and number with the noun which they describe. The feminine form of most adjectives is formed by adding **-e** to the end of the word. The consonant at the end of a word, usually silent in the masculine form, is pronounced when the word becomes feminine.

Ex: *Masculine*
le livre vert
(the green book)
luh <u>leev</u>-ruh vayr

Feminine
la pomme verte
(the green apple)
lah <u>puhm</u>-muh <u>vayr</u>-tuh

In the plural, adjectives, as in the case of nouns, take an **-s** (which is silent) at the end of the word.

POSSESSIVE ADJECTIVES

In French, possessive adjectives agree in number and gender with the noun they refer to:

masc. sing.	fem. sing.	masc. fem. plural		
mon	ma	mes	my	mohn/mah/meh
ton	ta	tes	your (familiar)	tohn/tah/teh
son	sa	ses	his/her/its	sohn/sah/seh
notre	notre	nos	our	<u>noh</u>-truh/noh
votre	votre	vos	your (formal)	<u>voh</u>-truh/voh
leur	leur	leurs	their	lehr

PERSONAL PRONOUNS

Subject

je	I	juh
tu	you (familiar)	too
vous	you (formal)	voo
il	he/it	eel
elle	she	ehl
nous	we	noo
vous	you	voo
ils/elles	they	eel/ehl

DIRECT/INDIRECT OBJECTS PRONOUNS

me/moi	me	muh/moo-ah
te/toi	you (familiar)	tuh/too-ah
vous	you (formal)	voo
le/lui	him	luh/loo-ee
la/elle	her	lah/ehl
nous	us	noo
vous	you (plural)	voo
eux,elles/leur	them (masc, fem)	eh/ehl/lehr

In French, the subject precedes the verb in the affirmative and negative, but follows the verb in the interrogative form.

Ex : **Je parle anglais.** (I speak English.)
juh pahl ahn-<u>glay</u>.
Je ne parle pas français. (I don't speak French.)
juh nuh pahl pah frahn-<u>say</u>.
Parlez-vous anglais? (Do you speak English?)
pahl-lay-<u>voo</u> anh-<u>glay</u>?

Pronouns precede the verb, except in imperative statements:

Ex : **Nous la connaissons.** (We know her.)
noo lah kohn-nehs-<u>sohn</u>
Ecoutez-le. (Listen to him.)
ay-koo-<u>tay</u>-luh

VERBS

Verbs in French are conjugated in the following way, depending on whether the infinitive form ends in **-er**, **-ir**, **-oir** or **-re**:

Simple Present:

Parler (to speak) *pahl-<u>lay</u>*		**Recevoir** (to receive) *ruh-suhv-<u>wahr</u>*	
je	parle	je	reçois
tu	parles	tu	reçois
il/elle	parle	il/elle	reçoit
nous	parlons	nous	recevons
vous	parlez	vous	recevez
ils/elles	parlent	ils/elles	reçoivent

Finir (to finish)
fee-neer

je	finis
tu	finis
il/elle	finit
nous	finissons
vous	finissez
ils/elles	finissent

Répondre (to answer)
ray-pohn-druh

je	réponds
tu	réponds
il/elle	répond
nous	répondons
vous	répondez
ils/elles	répondent

Simple Past:

j'ai	parlé
tu as	parlé
il/elle a	parlé
nous avons	parlé
vous avez	parlé
ils/elles ont	parlé

j'ai	reçu
tu as	reçu
il/elle a	reçu
nous avons	reçu
vous avez	reçu
ils/elles ont	reçu

j'ai	fini
tu as	fini
il/elle a	fini
nous avons	fini
vous avez	fini
ils/elles ont	fini

j'ai	répondu
tu as	répondu
il/elle a	répondu
nous avons	répondu
vous avez	répondu
ils/elles ont	répondu

IRREGULAR VERBS

Irregular verbs are numerous in French. Below you will find the conjugations for the two auxiliary verbs *être* (to be) and *avoir* (to have) as well as the verbs *aller* (to go) and faire (to make or to do), all irregular.

être (to be)
eh-truh

je	suis
tu	es
il/elle	est
nous	sommes
vous	êtes
ils/elles	sont

avoir (to have)
ahv-wahr

j'	ai
tu	as
il/elle	a
nous	avons
vous	avez
ils/elles	ont

aller (to go)
ahl-lay

je	vais
tu	vas
il/elle	va
nous	allons
vous	allez
ils/elles	vont

faire (to make or to do)
fehr

je	fais
tu	fais
il/elle	fait
nous	faisons
vous	faites
ils/elles	font

New Year's Day	**Jour de l'an** *joor duh-lahn*
Good Friday	**Vendredi saint** *vahn-druh-dee sehn*
Easter	**Pâques** *pahk*
Easter Monday	**Lundi de Pâques** *lehn-dee duh pahk*
Ascension Day	**Ascension** *ah-sahn-see-ohn*
Pentecoste	**Pentecôte** *pahn-tuh-koht*
Pentecoste Monday	**Lundi de Pentecôte** *luhn-dee duh pahn-tuh-koht*
May Day (May 1st)	**Premier mai** *pray-mee-ay may*
Victory Day (May 8th)	**8 mai** *oo-ee may*
Bastille Day (July 14th)	**14 juillet** *khah-tohr-zuh joo-ee-yuh-ay*
Assumption (August 15th)	**Assomption** *ahs-sohm-see-ohn*
All Saints (November 1st)	**Toussaint (1er novembre)** *toos-sehn (pruh-mee-ay noh vahm-bruh)*
Christmas	**Noël** *noh-ehl*
New Year's Eve	**Saint Sylvestre** *sehn seel-vehs-truh*

We reserved a room in the name of…

Nous avons réservé une chambre au nom de…
noo-zah-<u>vohn</u> ray-zehr-<u>vay</u> oon <u>shahm</u>-bruh oh noh duh…

Could you send up my bags?

Vous pouvez faire monter mes bagages?
voo poo-<u>vay</u> fehr mohn-<u>tay</u> meh bah-<u>gaj</u>?

What time is breakfast/lunch/dinner served?

A quelle heure est servi le petit déjeuner/déjeuner/dîner?
ah <u>kehl</u> ehr-ruh eh sehr-<u>vee</u> luh puh-<u>tee</u> day-juh-<u>nay</u>/luh day-juh-<u>nay</u>/luh dee-<u>nay</u>?

Could we have breakfast in our room at…?

Est-ce qu'on peut avoir le petit déjeuner dans la chambre à…?
ess-<u>kohn</u> puht ahv-<u>wahr</u> luh puh-<u>tee</u> day-juh-<u>nay</u> dahn lah <u>shahm</u>-bruh ah…

May I have my key?

Puis-je avoir ma clé?
pwee-juh ahv-<u>wahr</u> mah klay?

Put it on my bill.

Mettez-le sur ma note.
may-tay-<u>luh</u> suhr mah noht.

May I have a line please?

Puis-je avoir la ligne, s'il vous plaît?
pwee-juh ahv-<u>wahr</u> lah <u>leen</u>-yuh, seel-voo-<u>pleh</u>?

May I have another blanket/pillow?

Puis-je avoir une autre couverture/un autre coussin?
pwee-juh ahr-<u>wahr</u> oon <u>oh</u>-truh koo-vehr-<u>toor</u>/ oon <u>oh</u>-truh koo-<u>sayn</u>?

I closed the door to my room and left the keys inside.

J'ai fermé la porte de ma chambre en laissant les clés à l'intérieur.
jay fehr-<u>may</u> lah pohrt duh mah <u>shahm</u>-bruh ahn lehss-<u>ahn</u> leh klay ah-lahn-tay-ree-<u>ohr</u>.

I would like to reserve a single/double room.	**Je voudrais réserver une chambre simple/double.** *juh voo-dray ray-zehr-vay oon shahm-bruh saym-pluh/doo-bluh.*
I'd like a room with breakfast/half-board/full-board.	**Je voudrais une chambre avec petit déjeuner/en demi-pension/en pension complète.** *juh voo-dray oon shahm-bruh ah-vehk puh-tee day-juh-nay/ahn duh-mee pahn-see-ohn/ahn pahn-see-ohn kohm-pleht.*
What are your rates per day/per week?	**Quels sont vos prix par jour/par semaine?** *kehl-sohn voh pree pahr joor/pahr suh-mehn?*
Is breakfast included?	**Le petit déjeuner est compris?** *luh puh-tee day-juh-nay eh kohm-pree?*
We are staying three nights from... to...	**Nous resterons trois nuits du... au...** *noo rehs-tuh-rohn trwah noo-wee doo... oh...*
We will arrive at...	**Nous arriverons à...** *nooz ah-ree-vay-rohn ah...*

Things to remember

In French currency the 500 franc bill is the largest
denomination. Smaller bills are 200, 100, 50 and 20
francs. Coins come in 5, 10, 20, and 50 centimes, and
then 1, 2, 5, 10 and 20 franc pieces.

I don't have enough money.	**Je n'ai pas assez d'argent.** *jun nay pahz-ah-say dahr-jahn.*
Do you have change?	**Vous avez de la monnaie?** *vooz-ah-vay duh lah mohn-nay?*
Could you give me change for a 500 franc bill?	**Vous pouvez me faire de la monnaie sur un billet de cinq cents francs?** *voo-poo-vay muh fayr duh lah mohn-nay soor ayn bee-yay duh sahn frahn?*
I'd like to change these dollars /pounds into francs.	**Je voudrais changer ces dollars/livres en francs.** *juh voo-dray shahn-jay say doh-lahr/lee-vruh ahn frahn.*
What's the exchange rate for dollars/pounds?	**A combien est le change pour les dollars/livres?** *ah kom-bee-ehn eh luh shahnj poor lay doh-lahr/lay lee-vruh*

0	**zéro** *zay-roh*	13	**treize** *trehz*	50	**cinquante** *sehn-kahnt*
1	**un** *ayn*	14	**quatorze** *kah-tohrz*	60	**soixante** *soo-wah-sahnt*
2	**deux** *duh*	15	**quinze** *kehnz*	70	**soixante-dix** *soo-wah-sahn-dees*
3	**trois** *troo-wah*	16	**seize** *sehz*	80	**quatre-vingts** *kah-truh-vayn*
4	**quatre** *kah-truh*	17	**dix-sept** *dee-seht*	90	**quatre-vingt-dix** *kah-truh-vayn-dees*
5	**cinq** *sehnk*	18	**dix-huit** *dees-oo-eet*	100	**cent** *sahn*
6	**six** *sees*	19	**dix-neuf** *dees-nuhf*	101	**cent-un** *sahn-ayn*
7	**sept** *seht*	20	**vingt** *vayn*	110	**cent-dix** *sahn-dees*
8	**huit** *oo-eet*	21	**vingt et un** *vayn-ay-ayn*	200	**deux cents** *duh-sahn*
9	**neuf** *nuhf*	22	**vingt-deux** *vayn-duh*	300	**trois cents** *troo-wah-sahn*
10	**dix** *dees*	23	**vingt-trois** *vayn-troo-wah*	1000	**mille** *meel*
11	**onze** *ohnz*	30	**trente** *trahnt*	2000	**deux mille** *duh-meel*
12	**douze** *dooz-zuh*	40	**quarante** *kah-rahnt*	1 000 000	**un million** *ayn meel-ee-yohn*

1st	**premier/première** *pruh-mee-ay*	5th	**cinquième** *s ehn-kee-ehm*	9th	**neuvième** *nuh-vee-ehm*
2nd	**deuxième** *duhz-ee-ehm*	6th	**sixième** *seez-ee-ehm*	10th	**dixième** *deez-ee-ehm*
3rd	**troisième** *troo-wah-zee-ehm*	7th	**septième** *seht-ee-ehm*		
4th	**quatrième** *kah-tree-ehm*	8th	**huitième** *oo-eet-ee-ehm*		

Things to remember

French pastry shops (pâtisseries) *produce and sell a great variety of tempting sweets, all of excellent quality. So, don't hesitate to indulge (at least a little...) selecting the most typical ones from each region.*

What's this cake called?	**Comment s'appelle ce gâteau?** *kohn-mahn sah-pehl suh gah-toh?*
What's in this pastry?	**Qu'est-ce qu'il y a dans ce gâteau?** *kehs-keel-ee-ah dahn suh gah-toh?*
I'd like an assortment of pastries.	**Je voudrais un assortiment de pâtisseries.** *juh voo-dray ayn ah-sohr-tee-mahn duh pah-tee-sree.*
I'd like an ice-cream cone at... Francs, vanilla and chocolate with/without whipped cream.	**Je voudrais un cornet à... francs, à la vanille et au chocolat avec/sans chantilly.** *juh voo-dray ayn kohr-nay duh glahs ah... frahn, ah lah vah-nee-yuh eh oh shoh-koh-lah ah-vehk/sahn shahn-tee-yuh-ee.*
How much is it/are they?	**Combien coûte-t-il/coûtent-ils?** *kohm-bee-ehn koot-teel/koot-teel?*
Is there any chocolate/custard/alcohol in these pastries?	**Y a-t-il du chocolat/de la crème/de l'alcool dans ces pâtisseries?** *ee-ah-teel doo shoh-koh-lah/duh lah krem/duh lahl-kohl dahn say pah-tee-sree?*

How much does it cost?	**Combien cela coûte-t-il?** _kohm-bee-ehn suh-lah koot-teel?_
May I pay by credit card?	**Je peux payer avec la carte de crédit?** _juh puh pay-yay ah-vehk lah kahrt duh kray-dee?_
Do you take checks/traveler's checks?	**Vous acceptez les chèques/les chèques de voyage?** _vooz-ah-seht-tay leh shehk/leh shehk duh voh-ee-yahj?_
Could you give me the receipt please?	**Vous pouvez me donner le reçu s'il vous plaît?** _voo poo-vay muh duh-nay luh ruh-soo, seel-voo-play?_
Is the service/VAT included?	**Le service est compris/la TVA est comprise?** _luh sehr-vees eh kohm-pree/lah tay-vay-ah eh kohm-preez?_
Do I have to pay in advance?	**Je dois payer d'avance?** _juh doo-wah pay-yay dah-vahn-suh?_
Do I have to leave a deposit?	**Je dois laisser un acompte?** _juh doo-wah lay-say ahn ah-kohnt?_
I think you've given me the wrong change.	**Je crois que vous vous êtes trompé en me rendant la monnaie.** _juh kroo-wah kuh voo-voz-eht trohm-pay ahn muh rahn-dahn luh mohn-nay._

Could you help me please?	**Pouvez-vous m'aider s'il vous plaît?** *poo-vay-voo may-day, seel-voo-play?*
What's wrong?	**Qu'est-ce-qu'il y a?** *kehs-keel-ee-ya?*
What's going on?	**Que se passe-t-il?** *kuh suh pahs-teel?*
I need help.	**J'ai besoin d'aide.** *jay buh-zoo-ayn deh-duh.*
I don't understand.	**Je ne comprends pas.** *juh nuh kohm-prahn pah.*
Do you speak English?	**Vous parlez anglais?** *voo pahl-lay ahn-glay?*
Could you repeat that, please?	**Vous pouvez répéter, s'il vous plaît?** *voo poo-vay ray-pay-tay, seel-voo-play?*
I don't have any money left.	**Je n'ai plus d'argent.** *juh nay ploo dahr-jahn.*
I can't find my son/ my daughter.	**Je ne trouve plus mon fils/ma fille.** *juh nuh troo-vuh ploo mohn fees/ mah fee-yuh.*
I'm lost.	**Je me suis perdu.** *juh muh soo-ee pehr-doo.*
Leave me alone!	**Laissez-moi tranquille!** *lay-say moo-wah trahn-keel-luh.*

In this guide, French words are followed by their pronunciation in italics. Foreign sounds have been transcribed to resemble English pronunciation as closely as possible in order to facilitate reading. The stressed syllable is underlined.

au, eau are pronounced as "long *o*" in English.
Ex: **niveau** (level)
nee-voh
haut (tall)
oh

The pronunciation of **c** undergoes various changes depending upon the letters that follow it :
1) Followed by **a/o/u** it becomes "hard" as in "cat."
This sound, for pronunciation's sake, is represented by *k*:
Ex: **contrat** (contract)
kohn-trah
2) Followed by **h** + vowel it is pronounced as *sh* followed by *i and e*. This sound will thus be represented as *sh*:
Ex: **champagne**
shahm-pahn-yuh
3) Followed by **e** and **i** it is pronounced as *s* in English:
Ex: **cerise** (cherry)
seh-reez
4) **ç** is pronounced as a "voiceless *s*" in English:
Ex: **garçon** (boy)
gar-sohn

5) The so-called "nasals," typical of the French language, are difficult to pronounce for English speakers. We have attempted to make their transcription as simple as possible:
Ex: **banque** (bank)
bahnk

vin (wine)
vayn
ronde (round)
rohnd
un (one)
ayn

eil, eille are pronounced as the *ay* as in "may" in English:
Ex: **soleil** (sun)
soh-<u>leh</u>-ee-yuh
bouteille (bottle)
boo-<u>teh</u>-ee-yuh

g is pronounced as the "hard g" in English when followed by
a/o/u:
Ex: **gare** (station)
gahr
gorge (throat)
gohrj
guichet (ticket window)
ghee-<u>sheh</u>

g followed by **e** and **i** takes a round, sibilant sound that is
uncommon in English. However, through exposure to the
many French words used in English, we have become
familiar with this type of sound. It will be represented by *j*:
Ex: **abat-jour** (lampshade)
ah-bah-<u>joor</u>

e is pronounced by a very "close e" sound which will be
indicated by *uh*:
Ex: **lieu** (place)
lee-<u>euh</u>
je (I)
juh

The group **ill** has a very special sound comparable to the sound
yie as in *yield*. This pronunciation will be indicated by: *ee-yuh*.
Ex: **famille** (family)
fah-<u>mee</u>-yuh

The pronunciation of **oeu** is obtained by forming a sound in between long *o* and short *e* which we will represent by *ehr-ruh*:

Ex: **sœur** (sister)
<u>*sehr*</u>-*ruh*

r has the famous French guttural sound.

u has a "close sound" similar to the *oo* in "goose," and will be represented by *oo:*

Ex: **une** (oon)
oon

In general, if a word ends in a consonant, the consonant is silent. If the consonant is followed by a vowel, it is then pronounced.

Ex: **grand** *grahn*   (tall/masculine)
   grande *grahnd* (tall/feminine)

In French, unlike in English, accents are frequently used as important indications of how to pronounce vowels. The vowel **e**, for example, may have an "open" or "close" sound, depending upon the accent used (either "grave" as in **è**, or "acute" as in **é**).

Ex: **lièvre** (hare)
   lee-<u>ehv</u>-ruh   (with an "open" sound indicated with the "grave" accent and pronounced as *ai* in "air")

Ex: **début** (beginning)
   day-<u>boo</u>   (with a "close" sound indicated with the acute accent and pronounced as *ay* in "way")

In French pronunciation there are often *liaisons* or links between two words which will then be slurred together as if they were one. This may happen particularly in interrogatives when a word ends in a consonant and the following word begins with a vowel. In this case, the consonant becomes hard and links to the vowel that follows it:

Ex: **Où peut-on manger?** (Where can we have a meal?)
   oo puh-tohn mahn-jay?

   Quelle heure est-il? (What time is it?)
   kehl-ehr-ruh eh-teel?

The letter **s** behaves similarly in French as in English and may have a "voiceless" sound, as in the English word "sand," or a "voiced" sound as in the word "pose." To distinguish between these two pronunciations in French, we will represent the "voiceless" **s** by a single *s*, and the "voiced" **s** by a *z*.

Ex: **maison** (house)
   meh-zohn

A hint: If you ever have real difficulty making yourself understood in a particular situation, show your listener the phrase or word in writing.

Where are the restrooms please?	**Où sont les toilettes, s'il vous plaît?** *oo sohn leh toh-yeh-<u>leht,</u> seel-voo-<u>play</u>?*
Are they pay toilets?	**Les toilettes sont payantes?** *lay toh-yah-<u>leht</u> sohn pay-<u>yahnt</u>?*
There isn't any toilet paper, soap/aren't any paper towels.	**Il n'y a pas de papier toilette, savon/ essuie-mains.** *eel-nee-yah-<u>pah</u> duh pah-pee-<u>yay</u> toh-yeh-<u>leht</u>/duh sah-<u>vohn</u>/dehs-soo-ee <u>mayn</u>*
Are there toilets for the handicapped?	**Est-ce qu'il y a des toilettes pour handicapés.** *ehs-keel-ee-<u>yah</u> day toh-yeh-<u>leht</u> poor ahn-dee-kah-<u>pay</u>?*
The toilets are out of order.	**Le WC est bouché.** *luh vay-<u>say</u> eh boo-<u>shay</u>.*

Things to remember

In France smoking is forbidden in all public places
(museums, cinemas, etc.) and on public transportation
(subways, buses, etc.), except on trains that have a
special smokers' compartment. Generally smoking is not
allowed in restaurants unless there is a special section for
smokers indicated.

Is smoking allowed here?	**Est-ce qu'on peut fumer ici?** *ehs-<u>kohn</u> puh foo-<u>may</u> ee-<u>see</u>?*
Do you mind if I smoke?	**Cela vous dérange si je fume?** *seh-<u>lah</u> voo day-<u>rahnj</u> see juh <u>foo</u>-muh?*
May I have an ashtray?	**Je peux avoir un cendrier?** *juh puh ahv-wahr ayn sahn-dree-ay?*
Do you any matches?	**Vous avez des allumettes?** *vooz-ah-<u>vay</u> dayz-ah-loo-<u>meh</u>-tuh?*
Do you have a light?	**Vous avez du feu?** *vooz-ah-<u>vay</u> duh fuh?*
Would you mind putting out your cigarette/cigar?	**Cela vous ennuierait d'éteindre votre cigarette/cigare?** *suh-<u>lah</u> vooz-ah-noo-ee-<u>ray</u> day-<u>tehn</u>-druh <u>voh</u>-truh see-gah-<u>rayt</u>/see-<u>gahr</u>?*

Could you please call me a taxi?	**Vous pouvez m'appeler un taxi, s'il vous plaît?** *voo poo-vay mah-play ayn takh-see, seel-voo-play?*
To the main station/ to the airport.	**A la gare centrale/à l'aéroport.** *ah lah gahr sahn-trahl/ah-lay-roh-pohr.*
Please take me to this address/ this hotel.	**Conduisez-moi à cette adresse/à cet hôtel s'il vous plaît.** *kohn-doo-ee-zay-moo-wah ah seht ah-drehs/ah seht oh-tehl, seel-voo-play.*
Is it far?	**C'est loin?** *say loo-ayn?*
I'm really in a hurry.	**Je suis très pressé.** *juh soo-ee treh preh-say.*
Could you wait here a few minutes?	**Pouvez-vous attendre ici quelques instants?** *poo-vay-voo ah-tahn-druh ee-see kehl-kuhz ayns-tahn?*
How much will it cost?	**Ça va coûter combien?** *sah vah koo-tay kohm-bee-ehn?*
Please stop here/ at the corner.	**Arrêtez-vous ici/au coin, s'il vous plaît.** *ah-ray-tay-voo ee-see/oh koo-ayn, seel-voo-play.*
How much does that come to?	**Ça fait combien?** *sah fay kohm-bee-ehn?*
May I have a receipt?	**Vous pouvez me donner un reçu?** *Voo-poo-vay muh dohn-nay ayn ruh-soo?*
Keep the change.	**Gardez la monnaie.** *gahr-day lah mohn-nay.*

Things to remember

> To use pay phones in France, it is best to buy a telephone
> card since very few telephones accept coins anymore. If
> you do happen to find a phone that does, you will need
> coins of 1, 2 and 5 francs. Two types of telephone cards,
> one at about 40 francs, and the other at 96 francs are on
> sale in cafés, tobacconists' shops or from automatic
> dispensers. The minimum cost of a call is 2 francs.

Is there a phone?	**Est-ce qu'il y a un téléphone?** *ehs-keel-ee-<u>yah</u> ayn tay-lay-<u>fohn</u>?*
May I have a line?	**Puis-je avoir la ligne?** *pwee-juh ahv-<u>wahr</u> lah <u>leen</u>-yuh?*
I'd like a telephone card for 40/96 francs.	**Je voudrais une carte de téléphone à 40/96 francs.** *juh voo-<u>dray</u> oon kahrt duh tay-lay-<u>fohn</u> ah kah-<u>rahnt</u>/kah-truh-<u>vayn</u>-see frahn*
I'd like to make a call.	**Je voudrais téléphoner.** *juh voo-<u>dray</u> tay-lay-foh-<u>nay</u>.*
The number is…	**Le numéro est…** *luh noo-may-<u>roh</u> eh…*
How much does it cost to call the United States/ Great Britain?	**Combien ça coûte pour téléphoner aux Etats-Unis/en Grande-Bretagne?** *kohm-bee-<u>ehn</u> sah koot poor tay-lay-foh-<u>nay</u> ohz ay-<u>tahz</u> oo-nee/ehn grahn bruh-<u>tahn</u>-yuh?*
I can't get through.	**Je n'arrive pas à obtenir la communication.** *juh nah-<u>reev</u> pah ah ohb-tuh-<u>neer</u> lah koh-moo-nee-kah-see-<u>ohn</u>.*
What's the prefix for…	**Quel est l'indicatif pour…** *<u>kehl</u>-eh layn-dee-kah-<u>teef</u> poor…*

Hello, this is… speaking.	**Allô, …. à l'appareil.** *ah-loh…ah lah-pah-reh-yuh.*
May I speak to…	**Pourrais-je parler à…** *poo-ray-juh pahr-lay ah…?*
Sorry, I've dialed the wrong number.	**Excusez-moi je me suis trompé de numéro.** *ehs-koo-zay-moo-wah, juh muh soo-ee trohm-pay duh noo-may-roh*
This connection is very bad.	**La ligne est mauvaise.** *ah leen-yuh eh moh-vehz*

SOME TELEPHONE EXPRESSIONS:

Allô, qui est à l'appareil? *ah-loh, kee eht-ah lah-pah-reh-yuh?*	Hello, who's speaking?
Ne quittez pas. *nuh keet-tay pah.*	Please hold the line.
Rappelez plus tard, s'il vous plaît. *rah-puh-lay ploo tahr, seel-voo-play.*	Please call back later.
A la maison/ il-elle n'est pas là. *ah-lay meh-zohn eel-ehl neh pah lah.*	He/She isn't at home.
Vous vous êtes trompé de numéro. *voo-vooz-eht trohm-pay duh noo-may-roh.*	You have the wrong number.
Avez-vous un annuaire? *ah-vay-voo ayn ah-nuh-wayr?*	Do you have a directory?
Je voudrais téléphoner en PCV. *juh voo-dray tay-lay-foh-nay ehn pay-say-vay.*	I'd like to make a collect call.

What time is it?	**Quelle heure est-il?** *kehl ehr-r eh-teel?*
It's…	**Il est…** *eel eh…*
8 A.M./P.M.	**Huit heures du matin/du soir** *oo-eet ehr-r duh mah-tayn/doo* *soo-wahr*
8:00	**huit heures** *oo-eet ehr-r*
8:05	**huit heures cinq** *oo-eet ehr-r sehnk*
8:10	**huit heures dix** *oo-eet ehr-r dees*
8:15	**huit heures et quart** *oo-eet ehr-r ay khar*
8:20	**huit heures vingt** *oo-eet ehr-ruh vayn*
8:25	**huit heures vingt-cinq** *oo-eet ehr-ruh vayn-saynk*
8:30	**huit heures et demie** *oo-eet ehr-ruh ay duh-mee*
8:35	**neuf heures moins vingt-cinq** *nuhf ehr-ruh moo-ayn vayn-saynk*
8:40	**neuf heures moins vingt** *nuhf ehr-ruh moo-ayn vayn*
8:45	**neuf heures moins le quart** *nuhf ehr-ruh moo-ayn luh khar*

8:50	**neuf heures moins dix** *nuhf ehr-ruh moo-ayn dees*
12:00	**midi** (noon) *mee-dee*
"	**minuit** (midnight) *mee-noo-ee*
What time do you open/close?	**A quelle heure ouvrez-vous/fermez-vous?** *ah kehl ehr-ruh oo-vray-voo/ fehr-may-voo?*
What time does the restaurant close?	**A quelle heure ferme le restaurant?** *ah kehl ehr-r fehrm luh reh-stoh-rahn?*
What time do the stores close?	**A quelle heure ferment les magasins?** *ah kehl ehr-r fehrm lay mah-gah-sayn?*
How long does it take to get there?	**Combien de temps faudra-t-il pour y arriver?** *kohm-bee-ehn duh tahm foh-drah-teel poor ee ah-ree-vay?*
We arrived early/late.	**Nous sommes arrivés tôt/tard.** *noo-sahm-zah-ree-vay toh/tahr*
It's early/late.	**Il est tôt/tard.** *eel ay toh/tahr*
What time does the bus leave?	**A quelle heure part l'autobus?** *ah kehl ehr-ruh pahr loh-toh-boos-uh?*
The table is reserved for... this evening.	**La table est réservée pour... ce soir** *lah tah-bluh ay ray-zehr-vay poor... ehr-ruh suh soo-wahr.*

Things to remember

In France, as in practically every country in the world, it is customary to tip in restaurants, hotels, when you take a taxi, or at the hairdresser's, etc. Generally, tips are in proportion to the bill (from 5 to 10% of the total).

I'm sorry, but I don't have any change.	**Je suis désolé, je n'ai pas de monnaie.** *juh soo-ee day-zoh-lay, juh-nay-pah duh moh-nay*
Keep the change.	**Gardez la monnaie.** *gahr-day lay moh-nay.*
Round it off to... Francs.	**Arrondissez à... francs.** *ah-rohn-dee-say ah... frahn.*
Could you give me the change for...	**Vous pouvez me donner... en monnaie?** *voo poo-vay muh doh-nay... ahn moh-nay?*

Half a liter of…	**Un demi-litre de…**
	ayn deh-mee lee-tr duh
A liter of…	**Un litre de…**
	ayn lee-tr duh
A kilo of…	**Un kilo de…**
	ayn kee-loh duh
A half kilo (pound) of…	**Une livre de…**
	oon lee-vr duh
A hundred grams of…	**Cent grammes de…**
	sahn grah-m duh
A slice of…	**Une tranche de…**
	oon trahn-s duh
A portion of…	**Une portion de…**
	oon pohr-see-ohn duh
A dozen of…	**Une douzaine de…**
	oon doo-zehn duh
Ten francs of…	**Dix francs de…**
	dee frahn duh

GASTRONOMIC
DICTIONARY

au moins at least
au revoir good-bye
abats giblets, offal
abbaye f abbey
abondance See Cheeses p. 10
abonné(e) subscriber
abonnement m subscription
abri m shelter
abricot m apricot
absent(e) absent
abus m abuse, misuse
accepter to accept
accès m access
accessoires mpl accessories
accompagné(e) accompanied
accueil m reception
achats mpl purchases
acheter to buy
acompte m deposit
actionner to activate, to drive
addition f bill, check
adresse m address
adresser to address, to send
adulte m/f adult
aéroport m airport
affaires fpl affairs, business
affiche f poster
afin de in order to
âge m age
agence de voyage f travel agency
agent de police m policeman
agneau m lamb

agneau de lait m suckling lamb
agréable pleasurable, nice
agrumes mpl citrus fruiit
aigre-doux sweet-and-sour See Sauces, p. 73
aider to help
aiglefin m haddock
aigre sour
aiguillettes de saumon Turenne See Regional Dishes p. 46
ail m garlic
aïoli See Sauces, p. 73 and Regional Dishes, p. 54
air m air; **air conditionné**; air conditioned
aire f area; **aire de jeux** recreation area
airelle fpl bilberry
alcool m alcohol
alcoolisé(e) alcoholic
algues fpl seaweed
aliment m food
alimentation f feeding, food
Allemagne f Germany
aller to go
aller-retour m round trip
aller simple m one-way (ticket)
allergie f allergy
allumé(e) lighted, lit
allumer to light
allumette f match

alose à l'oseille See National Dishes p. 21
alouettes sans tête, See National Dishes p. 21
Aloxe Corton See Wines p. 87
aloyau m sirloin
alsacien(ne) Alsatian
amande f almond; **pâte d'amandes** almond paste
amandine f pastry made with almonds
ambassade f embassy
amer (ère) bitter
américaine (à l') See Gastronomic Terms p. 81
américano aperitif similar to red vermouth
ami(e) m/f friend
amidon m starch
amuse-gueule mpl savory titbits
an m year
ananas m pineapple
ananas belle de Meaux See National Dishes p. 21
anchois m anchovy
ancien (ne) old
andouille See Cold Cuts p. 78
andouillette See Cold Cuts p. 78
aneth m dill
angélique f (herb) angelica

anglais(e) English
Angleterre England
anguille f eel
anguille persillée See National Dishes p. 21
animaux mpl animals
animaux admis/non admis animals allowed/not allowed
anis m anise
anis étoilé m star anise
anis vert m green anise
anisette See Liqueurs p. 18
année f year
anniversaire m birthday
annuaire m telephone list, directory
annulation f cancellation
annuler to cancel
antibiotique m antibiotics
A.O.C. See **appellation**
août August
telephone call
apéritif m aperitif, drink (before a meal)
appel téléphonique m
appeler to call (telephone)
appellation d'origine contrôlée (A.O.C.) Controlled Denomination of Origin
appétit m appetite
appoint m exact change
apporter to bring

apprécier to appreciate
appuyer to push, to lean
âpre harsh, bitter
Apremont See Wines p. 87
après after
après-midi m afternoon
Aquitaine Aquitaine region
arachide f peanut
Arbois See Wines p. 87
argent m money
Armagnac See Liqueurs p. 18
aromate m aromatic herb
aromatisé(e) aromatic, flavored
arôme m aroma
arrêt stop; **arrêt de métro, de bus** m subway station, bus stop
arrêter to stop
arrière back, behind
arrivage m delivery
arrivée f arrival
arriver to arrive
arroltz ta xingar See Regional Dishes p. 38
arrondissement m district (of a city)
artichaut m artichoke
artichauts violets à Barigoule See Regional Dishes p. 54
artisanal(e) handmade, artisanal
ascenseur m lift, elevator
asperge f asparagus

aspirine f aspirin
assaisonnement m seasoning
assaisonner to season
assez enough
assiette f plate
assiette anglaise See National Dishes p. 21
assiette de crudités See National Dishes p. 21
assis(e) seated **place assise** seat
Avocat Fermont See Regional Dishes p. 50
avoine oats
avoir to have **avoir besoin de** to need
avril April
assortiment m assortment
assurance f insurance
attacher to attach
attendre to wait
attentif attentive
auberge f inn
aubergine f eggplant
aucun(e) not any
au-delà beyond
aujourd'hui today
aurore See Sauces p. 73
aussi also
authentique authentic
autobus m bus
automne autumn
autoroute f highway
autour around

autre other
avalanche f avalanche
avaler to swallow
avant before
avec with
avertir to warn
aveugle blind
avion m airplane
avocat m avocado
avocat au crabe See National
  Dishes p. 22
avocat fermon See Regional
  Dishes p. 50

baba See National Dishes
  p. 22
baeckaoffa See Regional
  Dishes p. 36
bagages mpl luggage
baguette f French bread
baignade f swim (sea, lake…)
baignoire f bath tub
bal m dance
ballotine f chicken galantine
banane f banana
bande f strip
banlieue f suburb, outskirts
banque f bank
bar (fish) m bass
bar m bar
bar au beurre blanc See
  National Dishes p. 22
barbue m flounder
barman m bartender

**"baron" d'agneau à la
  limousine** See Regional
  Dishes p. 48
bas low; en bas below, at the
  bottom
basilic m basil
basquaise (à la) See
  Gastronomic Terms p. 81
bassin m basin
bavarois See National Dishes
  p. 22
bavette f bib, flank (cul.)
béarnaise See Sauces p. 73
beau/belle handsome,
  beautiful
beaucoup a lot
beaufort See Cheeses p. 10
Beaujolais See Wines p. 87
bécasse f woodcock
bécassine f snipe
béchamel See Sauces p. 73
beignets mpl doughnut
Belgique Belgium
bellevue See Gastronomic
  Terms p. 82
belon f Belon oyster
Bénédictine See Liqueurs p. 18
Bergerac See Wines p. 88
berlingots mpl type of sweet
besoin need
betterave f beet root
bette f beet
beurre m butter **beurre
  d'anchois/blanc/maître**

d'hôtel See Sauces p. 73
beurrer to butter
bibliothèque f library
bicyclette f bicyle
bien well
bientôt soon
bienvenu(e) welcome
bière f beer; **bière blonde** lager; **bière brune** brown ale; **bière pression** draught beer
bifteck m steak
bigarade See Sauces p. 74
bigarreau m bigaroon cherry
bigorneau m winkle (seafood)
bijouterie f jewelry
billet m ticket
birewecke See Regional Dishes p. 36
biscotte f dry toast
biscuit m biscuit
bisque f soup
bisque de homard See National Dishes p. 22
blanc(he) white
blanc d'œuf m egg white
blanche See Sauces p. 74
blanchisserie f laundry
blanquette See Gastronomic Terms p. 82
blanquette de veau See National Dishes p. 22
blé m wheat

bleu See Gastronomic Terms p. 82
bleu d'Auvergne See Cheeses p. 10
bleu de Bresse See Cheeses p. 11
bœuf m beef
bœuf à la mode See National Dishes p. 22
bœuf braisé braised beef
bœuf bourguignon See Regional Dishes p. 42
bœuf en daube See National Dishes p. 22
boire to drink
boisson f beverage
boîte f box; **boîte de nuit** nightclub
bolée f bowl(ful), cup
bon(ne) good
bon appétit! Have a good meal!
bonbon m candy
bonjour hello
bonsoir good evening
Bordeaux Clairet See Wines p. 88
bordelaise See Sauces p. 75
botte f boot
bouche f mouth
bouchée f mouthful
bouchées à la Reine See National Dishes p. 22 and Recipes p. 57

boucherie f butcher's shop
bouchon m cork
bouchon bordelais See Sweets p. 8
boucle d'oreille f earring
boudin noir/blanc See Cold Cuts p. 78
bougie f candle
bouilli(e) boiled
bouillabaisse See Regional Dishes p. 54
bouillir to boil
bouillon m broth
boulangère See Gastronomic Terms p. 82
boulangerie f bakery
boule f ball
boulette f meatball
boulette d'Avesnes See Cheeses p. 11
Bourgogne Aligoté See Wines p. 88
Bourgueil See Wines p. 88
bourguignonne See Sauces p. 74
bourride des pêcheurs See Regional Dishes p. 54
bouteille f bottle
bouton m button
bovin m bovine
braisé See Gastronomic terms p. 82
brandade See Gastronomic Terms p. 82

brandade de morue See National Dishes p. 23
brasserie f café
Bretagne Brittany
breton(ne) Breton
brie de Coulommiers See Cheeses p. 11
brie de Meaux See Cheeses p. 11
briocherie f shop selling rolls and buns
briser to break
britannique British
broc m pitcher
broccio See Cheeses p. 11
broche (cul.) f spit
brochet m pike (fish)
brochet à l'ardennaise See Regional Dishes p. 45
brochet à l'orléannaise See Regional Dishes p. 44
brochette f skewer, kebab
brocoli m broccoli
brosse f brush
bruit m noise
brûlant(e) burning, boiling
brûlé(e) burnt
brûler to burn
brune(e) dark, brunette
brut(e) crude; dry (cider, champagne)
bruyant(e) noisy
bugnes lyonnaises See Regional Dishes p. 55

bureau de tabac m
tobacconist's
buvette f refreshment stand

cabecou See Cheeses p. 11
Cabernet d'Anjou See Wines
p. 88
cabillaud m fresh cod
cabine téléphonique f phone
booth
cabinet m office
cabinet médical doctor's
office
cacahuète f peanut
cacao m cocoa
cacou See Regional Dishes
p. 36
café m coffee, **café crème**
coffee with milk; **café
décaféiné** decaffeinated
café express expresso; **café
long** weak coffee; **café en
poudre** instant coffee
café liégeois See National
Dishes p. 23
cafetière f percolator
caghuse See Regional Dishes
p. 52
Cahors See Wines p. 88
caille f quail
caillebotte See Cheeses p. 12
cailles aux raisins See
National Dishes p. 23
caisse f cashier's

caissière f cashier
calamar m squid
calendrier m calendar
calisson d'Aix See Sweets p. 11
calmant sedative
calme calm
calorie f calorie
Calvados See Liqueurs p. 18
camembert See Cheeses p. 12
camomille f camomile
campagne f countryside
canard m duck
canard à l'orange See
National Dishes p. 23
caneton m duckling
cannelets See
Regional Dishes p. 38
cannelle f cinnamon
cantal See Cheeses p. 12
câpres fpl capers
carafe f decanter
cardamone f cardomom
carnet m notebook
carotte f carrot
carpe f carp
carré (cul.) m loin
carré de l'est See Cheeses
p. 12
carrelet m plaice (fish)
carte d'identité f national ID
card
carte de crédit f credit card
carvi m caraway
cassé(e) broken

casse-noix m nutcracker
casser to break
casserole f saucepan
cassis m blackcurrant
cassolette f small baking dish
cassolette de pibales See
  Regional Dishes p. 38
cassonade raw brown sugar
cassoulet See National
  Dishes p. 23
cave f cellar
caviar m caviar
cèdre m cedar
céleri m celery; **céleri-rave**
  celeriac
cendre f ash
cendrier m ashtray
cent a hundred
central(e) central
centre m center
cèpe m boletus mushroom
cèpes à la bordelaise See
  Regional Dishes p. 38
céréale f cereal
cerfeuil m chervil
cerise f cherry
cerveau m brain
cervelas See Cold Cuts p. 78
cervelle f brain
chabichou See Cheeses p. 12
Chablis See Wines p. 89
chaise f chair; **chaise haute**
  highchair
chambre f room; **chambre**

double double room
  chambre simple single room
Champagne See Wines p. 89
champignon m mushroom
Champigny See Wines p. 89
change m exchange
changer to change
chanson f song
Chantilly See **crème**
  Chantilly
chaource See Cheeses p. 12
chapeau m hat
chapelure f breadcrumbs
chaque each, each one
charcuterie f delicatessan
chariot m cart
charlotte aux fraises See
  National Dishes p. 23
charlotte aux fruits See
  Recipes p. 58
charolais See Cheeses p. 12
Chartreuse See Liqueurs
  p. 18
chasseur See Gastronomic
  Terms p. 83 and Sauces
  p. 74
châtaigne f chestnut
châteaubriand à la moutarde
  See National Dishes p. 23
Châteauneuf-du-Pape See
  Wines p. 89
chaud(e) hot (temperature)
chaude aux câpres See
  Sauces p. 74

chaudrée des pêcheurs See Regional Dishes p. 53

chauffage m heating

chauffer to heat

chauffeur m driver

chausson aux pommes small puff pastry roll with apple filling

chef m cook

chemise f shirt

chèque m check

che(r)(ère) expensive

chevreau m kid

chevreuil m venison

chicorée f chicory

Chinon See Wines p. 89

chipirons farcis à l'encre See Regional Dishes p. 38

chipolata See Cold Cuts p. 78

chips f potato chips

chocolat m chocolate

chocolats mpl pieces of chocolate

chocolat liégeois See National Dishes p. 24

choix m choice; **desserts au choix** choice of desserts

chope f mug

chorizo See Cold Cuts p. 78

chose f thing

chou m cabbage; **chou vert** green cabbage; **chou-fleur** cauliflower

chou à la crème See National Dishes p. 24

chouchen See Liqueurs p. 18

choucroute garnie à l'alsacienne See National Dishes p. 24

chou de Bruxelles m Brussel sprouts

chou farci See National Dishes p. 24

ciboulette f chives

cidre See Liqueurs p. 19

citron m lemon

citronnade f lemonade

civet See Gastronomic Terms p. 83

civet de lapin See National Dishes p. 24

clafoutis See National Dishes p. 24

clair(e) clear, light

client(e) client, customer

clientèle f customers

climatisé(e) air conditioned

clou de girofle m clove

cochon m pig

cocktail de langoustines See National Dishes p. 24

cocotte f casserole, pot

cocotte-minute f pressure cooker

cœur m heart

Cognac See Liqueurs p. 19

coin m corner

cointreau brandy distilled from oranges

colorant m coloring

combien how much

commande f order

commander to command

comme as, like

commencer to begin

comment ça va ? How are you?

comment how, in what way; **comment t'appelles-tu ?** What's your name?

commerçant m shopkeeper

commerce m trade

compl(et)(ète) complete

compote f stewed fruit

comprendre to understand

comptant in cash

comptoir m counter

comté See Cheeses p. 13

concentré de tomates m tomato concentrate

concombre m cucumber

confirmer to confirm

confit See Gastronomic Terms p. 83

confiture f jam

confortable comfortable

congélateur m freezer

congelé(e) frozen

conservé(e) preserved

consommation f consumption

consommé See Gastronomic Terms p. 83

content(e) happy, satisfied

continuer to continue

contre against

contrôler to control

coq au vin See National Dishes p. 24

coque f eggshell

coquelet m cockerel

coquillage m seashell

coquille f shell

coquilles Saint-Jacques f scallops

coquilles Saint-Jacques à la normande See Regional Dishes p. 51

corail m coral

Corbières See Wines p. 89

coriandre f coriander

cornet de glace m ice-cream cone

cornichon m pickle

Corse Corsica

côte f rib **côte de bœuf** rib of beef

Côte d'Azur French Riviera

Côte de Beaune See Wines p. 89

Coteaux du Languedoc See Wines p. 89

Coteaux du Lyonnais See Wines p. 90

côtelette f (culin.) chop

Côtes de Bourg See Wines p. 90

Côtes de Brouilly See Wines p. 90

Côtes de Fronsac See Wines p. 90

Côtes de Nuit See Wines p. 90

Côtes de Provence See Wines p. 90

Côtes du Lubéron See Wines p. 90

Côtes du Rhône See Wines p. 90

Côtes-du-Roussillon See Wines p. 91

Côtes-du-Ventoux See Wines p. 91

côtes de porc à l'ardennoise See Regional Dishes p. 45

côtes de veau fromagères See Regional Dishes p. 24

coton m cotton

cou m neck

cou d'oie farci See Regional Dishes p. 49

couleur f color

coulis See Gastronomic Terms p. 83

coulommiers See Cheeses p. 13

coupe f cup, glass

couper to cut

courant (e) current

courge f marrow

courgette f zucchini

court-bouillon m simmering broth

couscous m couscous

coussin m cushion

coût m cost

couteau m knife

coûter to cost

coûteux (euse) costly

couvert m cover

couvrir to cover

crabe m crab

cravate f tie

crayon m pencil

crédit m credit **la maison ne fait pas de crédit** no credit is given here

crème (à la) See Gastronomic Terms p. 81

crème anglaise See Gastronomic Terms p. 83

crème au beurre See Gastronomic Terms p. 83

crème au vin de Sauternes/de Bordeaux See Regional Dishes p. 38

crème Chantilly See Gastronomic Terms p. 83

crème de cassis See Liqueurs p. 19

crème fouettée whipped cream

crème fraîche f fresh cream

crème frangipane See Gastronomic Terms p. 83
crème pâtissière See Gastronomic Terms p. 83
crème renversée See Gastronomic Terms p. 83
crêpes See National Dishes p. 83
crêpe bretonne See Regional Dishes p. 43
crépinettes See Cold Cuts p. 78
cresson m cresson
crevette f shrimp
croissant m croissant roll
croquant(e) crunchy
croquette f croquette
croque-monsieur See National Dishes p. 25
crottin de Chavignol See Cheeses p. 13
crottin de chèvre chaud See National Dishes p. 25
croustade See Gastronomic Terms p. 84
croustillant(e) crispy
croûte f crust
crouton m crouton
cru(e) raw
cru m vineyard ; **premier cru** wine of superior vintage **cru classé** classified wine
crudité f raw vegetable
crustacé m crustacean

cuiller/cuillère m/f spoon; **cuiller à café** teaspoon
cuire to cook
cuisine f cooking, kitchen
cuisinier (ère) m/f cook
cuisses de grenouilles au persil et au citron See National Dishes p. 25
cuisson f cooking
cuit(e) cooked
cumin m cummin
curcuma m tamarind
cure-dents m tooth picks

d'où êtes-vous? Where are you from?
dame f lady
dans in
danser to dance
darne f (fish) slice
darnes de turbot à la Bréval See Regional Dishes p. 50
datte f dates
daube See Gastronomic Terms p. 84
daurade f gilt-head
dé m cube
débit de boissons m beverage outlet
débiter to debit to produce
déboucher to uncork
début m beginning
décapsuleur m can opener
décembre December

décommander to cancel
décongeler defrost
décoration f decoration
décoré(e) decorated
décortiqué(e) to shell, to husk
dégraisser to skim the fat off
degré m degree
dégustation f tasting
dehors out, outside
déjeuner m lunch
délice de sandre au Riesling See Regional Dishes p. 37
demain tomorrow
demander to ask
demi half; **un demi (de bière)** half-pint of beer
demi-pension f half-board
dent f tooth
dentier m denture
déposer deposit, leave
dépôt m deposit; **dépôt de pain** place that sells bread
depuis since, from
dérangement m disturbance
déranger to disturb
dernier(ère) last
derrière behind, back
désinfectant m disinfectant
désinfecter to disinfect
désirer to desire
désolé(e) sorry
dessert m dessert
dessous under

dessus above, on top
devant in front of
devise (fin.) currency
devoir to have to
diabétique diabetic
diable (à la) See Sauces p. 74 and Gastronomic Terms p. 81
diabolo grenadine and mint with lemonade drink
différent(e) different
difficile difficult
digeste digestible
digestif m liqueur
dimanche Sunday
dinde aux marrons See National Dishes p. 25
dindon m turkey cock
dîner m dinner
dire to say
directeur m director
direction f management
distance f distance
distributeur m dispenser
donner to give
dorade See **daurade**
doré(e) golden
double double
douzaine f a dozen
dragée See Sweets p. 8
droit(e) straight
droite right
ducs See Cheeses p. 13
dur(e) hard

eau f water; **gazeuse** sparkling water; **minérale** mineral water

eau-de-vie f brandy

échalote f shallot

échelle f ladder, scale

économique economical

écorce f bark, peel

écrevisse f crawfish

écrevisses à la nage See National Dishes p. 25

écrire to write

édam français See Cheeses p. 13

Edelzwicker See Wines p. 91

édulcorant m sweetener

effacer to erase

églefin/aiglefin (cabillaud) m haddock

élevage m breeding

emmenthal français See Cheeses p. 13

en-cas m snack

en croûte See Gastronomic Terms p. 84

en gelée See Gastronomic Terms p. 84

en papillottes See Gastronomic Terms p. 84

enceinte pregnant

encore again

encornet m squid

endive f chicory

endives au jambon gratinées See National Dishes p. 25 and Recipes p. 59

enfant m/f child

enlever to remove

enrobé(e) covered, coated

ensemble together

ensuite afterwards, then

entier(ère) whole

Entre-deux-Mers See Wines p. 91

entrecôte à la bordelaise See Regional Dishes p. 38

entrecôte à la moelle See National Dishes p. 26

entrée f entrance, hors-d'oeuvre

entremets m cream dessert

entrer to enter

enveloppe f envelope

envie f desire, craving

environ about, approximately

épais(se) thick

épaule f shoulder

épaule d'agneau f pré-salé See Regional Dishes p. 52

épi de mais m ear of corn

épice f spice

épicé(e) spicy

épicerie f grocery shop

épinards mpl spinach

épinards à la crème See National Dishes p. 26

épingle à nourrice f safety pin

époisses See Cheeses p. 13
épouse f wife,
époux m husband
erreur f error
escabèche (à l') See
Gastronomic Terms p. 81
escalier stairs
escalope f escalope
escalope savoyarde See
Regional Dishes p. 55
**escalopes de veau
bohémienne** See National
Dishes p. 26
escargot m snail
**escargots à la
bourguignonne** See
Regional Dishes p. 42
espadon m swordfish
espèce f cash; **payer en
espèces** to pay in cash
essayer to try
estival summery
estomac m stomach
estouffade f stew
estragon m tarragon (à la)
See Sauces p. 74
esturgeon m surgeon
établissement m
establishment foundation
États-Unis d'Amérique
United States of America
été m summer
éteindre to turn off
étiquette f label

étouffée (à l') steamed,
braised
étranger (ère) foreigner
être en retard to be late
étroit(e) tight
évanoui(e) disappeared
fainted
éviter to avoid
excursion f day trip
excuse f excuse
expert(e) expert
express m espresso coffee
extérieur(e) exterior outside
externe outer
extrait(e) extracted

face f face **en face de**
opposite
facile easy
facture f invoice
faible weak
faim f hunger
faire to do, to make; **faire
attention** to be careful
faisan m pheasant
faisan au chou See National
Dishes p. 26
fait maison homemade
familial(e) domestic
familier familiar
famille f family
farce f stuffing
farci(e) stuffed
farine f flour

Faugères See Wines p. 91
faux-filet m sirloin
faux-filet à la Berrichone See
  Regional Dishes p. 44
femme f woman, wife
fenêtre f window
fenouil m fennel
férié holiday
ferme firm
fermé(e) closed
fermer closed
fermeture f closing
fermier m farmer
fête f party
feu m fire
Feuille de Dreux See
  Cheeses p. 14
feuilleté m puffed; flaky **pâte
  feuilletée** puffed pastry
fève f broadbean
février February
figue f figue
fil m thread
filet m fillet
filets de dorade à l'estragon
  See National Dishes p.
fille f girl
fillette f little girl
fils m son
fin(e) fine
fin de semaine at the end of
  the week
financière See Sauces p. 74
Fine See Liqueurs p. 19

fines herbes fpl aromatic
  herbs
finir to finish
Fitou See Wines p. 91
flambé(e) flambé
flageolets kidney beans
flamiche aux poireaux See
  Regional Dishes p. 52 and
  Recipes p. 60
flamme f flame
flammekueche See Regional
  Dishes p. 37
flan m flan
flétan m halibut
fleur f flower
flocon m flake
flûte de champagne f
  champagne flute glass
foie m liver
foie gras See Cold Cuts
  p. 79
**foie gras des Ducs de
  Lorraine** See Regional
  Dishes p. 48
**foie gras d'oie frais aux
  raisins** See Regional Dishes
  p. 39
fois f time(s)
foncé(e) dark
fonctionner to function, to
  work
fond m bottom; **fond
  d'artichaut** aritchoke heart
fonds d'artichauts à la

parisienne See National Dishes p. 26

fondue bourguignonne See National Dishes p. 26

forestière See Gastronomic Terms p. 84

fort(e) strong

fouettée (crème) whipped (cream)

four m oven

fourchette f fork

Fourme d'Ambert See Cheeses p. 14

fourré(e) filled

frais (fraîche) fresh

fraise f strawberry

fraise des bois f wild strawberry

fraises au Bordeaux See National Dishes p. 26

fraisier See National Dishes p. 26

framboise f raspberry

français(e) French

frangipane See National Dishes p. 27

friandise f delicacy, candy

fricassée See Gastronomic Terms p. 84

frites See National Dishes p. 27

friture f fry

froid(e) cold

fromage m cheese

fromage de tête See Cold Cuts p. 79

froment m wheat

Frontignan See Wines p. 92

fruit m fruit; **fruit confit** candied fruit; **fruit de mer** seafood; **fruit des bois** fruit of the forest (wild berries); **fruits frais** fresh fruit; **fruits secs** dried fruit

fruits déguisés See Sweets p. 8

fumé(e) smoked

fumer to smoke

fumet See Gastronomic Terms p.

fumeur smoker

galantine See Cold Cuts p. 79

galette f round, flat cake

galette des Rois See National Dishes p. 27

Gamay de Touraine See Wines p. 92

gambas m jumbo shrimp

gant m glove

garbure See Regional Dishes p. 39

garçon m boy, waiter

garde f guard
pharmacie/médecin de garde pharmacist/doctor on duty

garder to keep

garderie d'enfants f day nursery

gardien m keeper, caretaker (of building)

gare f station

garniture (cul.) f accompanying vegetables

garniture limousine See Regional Dishes p. 48

gâteau m cake

gâteau aux noix et au rhum See Regional Dishes p. 50

gâteau basque See Regional Dishes p. 39

gâteau breton See Regional Dishes p. 43

gaufre See Sweets p. 8

gaufrette f wafer

gazeux(euse) fizzy

gelée f jelly

genièvre m juniper

génoise f sponge cake

genre m type

gésiers confits See Cold Cuts p. 79

Gewürztraminer See Wines p. 92

gibelotte m See Gastronomic Terms p. 84

gibier m game

gigot m leg (of lamb)

gigot d'agneau au four See National Dishes p. 27

gingembre m ginger

girolle f chanterelle mushroom

glaçage m frosting

glace f ice-cream

glace aux noisettes See Regional Dishes p. 53

glace de viande meat glaze

glace Nelusko See Regional Dishes p. 44

glacier m ice-cream maker, ice-cream shop

glaçon m ice cube

gorge throat

gouda français See Cheeses p. 14

goujon m gudgeon (fish)

gourmand(e) to be avid for (food); to be fond of sweets

goût m taste

goûter to taste

goûter m snack

goutte f drop

gracieusement cordially, courteously

graine m

grand(e) big, great

grand Veneur See Sauces p. 74

Grande-Bretagne Great Britain

grande surface f supermarket

gras(se) fat

gratin (au) See Gastronomic Terms p. 82

gratin dauphinois See National Dishes p. 27
gratin de langoustines See Regional Dishes p. 53
gratin savoyard See Regional Dishes p. 56
gratiné(e) au gratin
graton See Cold Cuts p. 79
gratuit(e) free
Graves See Wines p. 92
grec(greque) Greek
Grèce Greece
grenade f pomegranate
grenadin m thick slice of veal
grenadine f grenadine
grenouille f frog **cuisses de grenouilles** frogs legs
gribiche See Sauces p. 75
gril f grill pan
grillade f grill
grillé See Gastronomic Terms p. 82
griotte f Morello cherry
grondin m gurnard (fish)
Gros Plant See Wines p. 92
groseille f red currant
groupe m group
guichet m ticket window, counter
guide f guide (book)
guinette f See Sweets p. 8

haché(e) minced, ground

hacher minced
halles fpl market
handicapé(e) handicapped
hareng m herring
harengs marinés See National Dishes p. 27
haricots blancs mpl haricot beans
haricots verts mpl French beans, stringbeans
hébergement m accomodation, lodging
herbes See **fines herbes**
Hermitage See Wines p. 92
heure f hour; **d'ouverture, de fermeture** opening time/closing time
hier yesterday
hiver m winter
hollandais(e) Dutch
hollandaise See Sauces p. 75
Hollande Holland
homard m lobster
homard à l'américaine See National Dishes p. 27
homme m man
homogénéisé(e) homogenized
hôpital m hospital
horaire m hours, timetable
hors-d'œuvre m appetizer, opener
hôtel m hotel
huile f oil

huître f oyster
huîtres chaudes au Calvados et à l'infusion de pommes See Regional Dishes p. 51

ici here
il fait chaud (weather) It's hot.
île flottante See National Dishes p. 27
imperméable m raincoat
important(e) important
impossible impossible
inclus(e) included
inconfortable uncomfortable
indicatif (téléphonique) dialing code
indications f pl direction
informations f pl news
informer to inform
inoffensi(f) (ive) harmless
insecte m insect
intégral complete
interdit forbidden
interne inner
interurbain interurban (telephone) long distance
intoxication alimentaire f food poisoning
introduire to introduce
inviter to invite
Irlande Ireland
Italie Italy

jamais never
jambe f leg
jambon See Cold Cuts p. 79
jambon de magret See Cold Cuts p. 79
janvier January
jardin garden
jardinière de légumes See National Dishes p. 27
jaune yellow; **jaune d'œuf** egg yolk
jeter to throw
jeudi Thursday
jeune m youngster
jouer to play
jour m day; **jour de l'an** New Year's Day; **jour ouvrable** weekday; **jour férié** holiday
journal m newspaper
journée f day
juillet July
juin June
julienne See Gastronomic Terms p. 84
Jura See Wines p. 92
jus m juice; **jus de fruits** fruit juice
jusqu'à until

kaki m kaki (fruit)
kir aperitif made with white wine and blackcurrant syrup
Kirsch See Liqueurs p. 19

kiwi m kiwi
kougelhopf See Regional Dishes p. 37

la caraque See Regional Dishes p. 54
la Clape See Wines p. 92
lac m lake
laid(e) ugly
laisser to leave
lait m milk
laitage m milk product
laitue m lettuce
lamproie f lamprey
lamproie à la bordelaise See Regional Dishes p. 39
langouste f crawfish, rock lobster
langoustine f Dublin Bay prawn, scampi
langoustines à l'aneth See Regional Dishes p. 50
langres See Cheeses p. 14
langue f tongue
langue de bœuf au bouillon See National Dishes p. 28
langue de chat See Sweets p. 8
lapereau m young rabbit
lapin m rabbit
lapin à la moutarde See National Dishes p. 28
lapin en gibelotte See National Dishes p. 28

lard m bacon
laurier m bay leaf
laver to wash
léger(ère) light (weight)
légume f vegetable
légumes verts mpl green vegetables
lentille f lentil
lequel, laquelle who, whom which
levain m leaven
lever un verre à la santé de quelqu'un (drink) to toast to someone
levure f yeast
libre free
lieu m place
lieu (fish) whiting
lièvre m hare
ligne f line, route
limande f lemon sole
limonade f lemonade
lire to read
lisse smooth
liste f list
livarot See Cheeses p. 14
livre m book
location f rental
loin far
lon(g) (gue) long
longe f loin
loup de la Méditerranée braisé au Ricard See Regional Dishes p. 47

lourd(e) heavy
loup de mer m seabass
lumière f light
lundi Monday
lunettes fpl glasses (to see)

macaron See Sweets p. 8
mâcher to chew
Mâcon See Wines p. 93
Mâcon-Villages See Wines
  p. 93
macrobiotique macrobiotic
madame f Mrs.
mademoiselle f Miss
madère See Sauces p. 75
Madiran See Wines p. 93
magasin m store
magret See Gastronomic
  Terms p. 84
magrets au poivre vert See
  National Dishes p. 28
mai May (month)
maigre lean
main f hand
mais m maize, corn
maison f house **fait maison**
  See Gastronomic Terms p. 84
mal m ache; **mal de tête**
  headache; **mal de ventre**
  stomachache
malade sick, ill
maladie f illness
malentendu m
  misunderstanding

Manche (la) English Channel
mandarine f tangerine
manger to eat
manteau m coat
maquereau m mackerel
marcassin m young wild
  boar
Marc de Bourgogne See
  Liqueurs p. 19
marchand m vendor
marché m market
marcher to walk
mardi Tuesday
marengo (poulet, veau) See
  National Dishes p. 31
margarine f margarine
Margaux See Wines p. 93
mari m husband
marinade See Gastronomic
  Terms p. 85
marinière See Gastronomic
  Terms p. 81
marjolaine f marjoram
maroilles See Cheeses p. 14
marron m chestnut
marron glacé See Sweets p. 8
mars March (month)
massepain m marzipan
matelote See Gastronomic
  Terms p. 85
**matelote d'anguilles à la
  lyonnaise** See Regional
  Dishes p. 56
matin m morning

mauvais(e) bad

mayonnaise f mayonnaise and See Sauces p. 75

méchant(e) mean, cruel

médaillons de veau "Bergerette" See Regional Dishes p. 46

médecin m doctor

médecine f medicine

Médoc See Wines p. 93

meilleur(e) best

mélange m mixture

melon m melon

même same

menthe f mint

menu m menu; **menu à prix fixe** fixed price menu; **menu touristique** tourist menu

mer f sea

merci thank you

mercredi Wednesday

mère f mother

merguez f See Cold Cuts p. 79

meringue f meringue

merlan m whiting

mérou m grouper

messieurs mpl men, gentlemen

métro m subway

mettre to put

mettre la table set the table

meunière See Gastronomic Terms p. 85

Meursault See Wines p. 93

mias (or **millas girondin**) See Regional Dishes p. 39

miel m honey

mieux better

mille thousand

mille-feuille See National Dishes p. 28

mimolette See Cheeses p. 14

Minervois See Wines p. 93

minute f minute

mirabelle f cherry plum See Liqueurs p. 19

moelle f marrow

moins less

mois m month

moitié f half

moka See National Dishes p. 28

mollusque m mollusc

monnaie f change

monsieur m gentleman, Mr.

mont-Blanc glacé See Regional Dishes p. 56

montant (à payer) m amount (to pay)

monter to climb

montrer to show

monument m monument

morceau m piece

morille f morel mushroom

mornay See Sauces p. 75

morue f cod

mot m word

mou (molle) limp, soft
mouche f fly (insect)
mouchoir m handkerchief
mouclade See National
Dishes p. 28
moules f mussels
moules marinière See
National Dishes p. 28
moulin à poivre m pepper
mill
mousse de foie See
Cold Cuts p. 80
mousse de saumon See
National Dishes p. 29
mousseux(euse) frothy,
sparkling
moustique m mosquito
moutarde f mustard See
Sauces p. 75
mouton m mutton
moyen de transport m means
of transportation
mulet (cul.) m mullet
munster See Cheeses p. 15
mûr(e) mature, ripe
mur m wall
muscade f nutmeg
Muscadet See Wines p. 93
Muscat See Wines p. 94
musée m museum
musique f music
muxuk See Regional Dishes
p. 39
myrtille f bilberry

nage (à la) See Gastronomic
Terms p. 81
nager to swim
nantua See Sauces p. 75
nappe f tablecloth
nappé(e) sauce-covered
nature f nature
naturel(le) natural
navarin See Gastronomic
Terms p. 85
navarin d'agneau See
National Dishes p. 29
navet m turnip
navets glacés See National
Dishes p. 29
nécessaire necessary
négociant m merchant
neuchâtel See Cheeses p. 15
Noël Christmas
noir(e) black
noisette f hazelnut
noix f walnut; de cajou
cashew nut; de coco
coconut
nom de famille m surname
non-fumeur non-smoker
nord m north
normande (à la) See
Gastronomic Terms p. 81
nouilles fpl noodles
nourriture f food; busy
nouveau (nouvelle) new
novembre November
noyau m (fruit) stone, pit

nuit f night
numéro m number

objet m object
obligatoire obligatory
obtenir to obtain
occupé(e) occupied; engaged
octobre October
odeur f odor, smell
œil m eye
œuf m egg; **œufs à la coque**
  soft-boiled egg; **œufs
  brouillés** See National
  Dishes p. 29 **œuf dur** hard-
  boiled egg **œuf poché**
  poached egg **œuf sur le plat**
  fried egg
**œufs cocotte aux pointes
  d'asperges** See National
  Dishes p. 29 and Recipes
  p. 61
œufs en meurette See
  Regional Dishes p. 42
oie f goose
oignon m onion
oignons farcis See National
  Dishes p. 29
oiseau m bird
olive f olive
olivet cendré See Cheeses
  p. 15
omelette norvégienne See
  National Dishes p. 29
omelette soufflée à la

Verveine du Velay See
  Regional Dishes p. 47
**omelette soufflée, flambée
  au Rhum** See Regional
  Dishes p. 46
or m gold
orange pressée fresh orange
  juice
ordonnance f prescription
oreille f ear
orge m barley
orgeat m orgeat (syrup)
origan m oregano
ortolans rôtis See National
  Dishes p. 29
os m bone
oseille f sorrel
ôter to take off
où where
oublier to forget
oursin m sea urchin
ouvert(e) open
ouvre-boîte m can opener
ouvre-bouteilles m bottle
  opener
ouvrir to open

paiement m payment
**paillassons de pommes de
  terre** See National Dishes
  p. 29
pain m bread; **pain bis**
  brown bread; **pain de
  campagne** farmhouse bread;

pain au chocolat roll with chocolate filling; **pain complet** wholemeal bread; **pain d'épices** gingerbread See Sweets p. 8; **pain de mie** sandwich bread; **pain aux raisins** raisin roll
pair (number) even **impair(e)** odd
paire f pair
palourde f clam
pamplemousse m grapefruit
pamplemousse au crabe See National Dishes p. 30
pan-bagnat See Regional Dishes p. 54
pané(e) coated (breadcrumbs)
paner to coat
panne f breakdown
pansement m bandage
papier m paper
papiers mpl documents, ID
Pâques Easter
parapluie m umbrella
parc m park
parce que because
pardon sorry, excuse me
pareil(le) same
parfait(e) perfect
parfait au Cognac See National Dishes p. 30
parfum m perfume, flavor
Paris-Brest See National Dishes p. 30
partir to leave
passeport m passport
pastèque f watermelon
pastis See Liqueurs p. 19
pâté See Cold Cuts p. 80
pâte f pastry, mixture, dough, batter; **pâte brisée** shortcrust pastry; **pâte sablée** sablé pastry; **pâte feuilletée** puff or flaky pastry
pâtes pasta
pâtes à potage noodles
pâtisserie f pastry
patxaran (patcharane) See Liqueurs p. 19
Pauillac See Wines p. 94
paupiettes (cul.) See Gastronomic Terms p. 85
payer to pay; **payer comptant** to pay cash
pays m country
paysan(ne) countryman, farmer, peasant
peau f skin
pêche f fishing
Pêche Melba See National Dishes p. 30
peler to peel
Pelure d'Oignon See Wines p. 94
perche (cul.) perche (fish)
perdre to lose
perdrix f partridge

perdrix au chou See National Dishes p. 30

périgueux See Sauces p. 75

Pernod aperitif made with anise

persil m parsley

personne f nobody, no one, a person

pétillant(e) fizzy, sparkling

petit(e) small, little

petit déjeuner m breakfast

petit-fours See Sweets p. 9

petit salé aux lentilles See National Dishes p. 30

petite marmite des montagnards ariégeois See Regional Dishes p. 47

petit pois m peas

pets-de-nonne See Sweets p. 9

peu f (quantity) not much, a little

pharmacie f chemist's; pharmacy; **de garde** on duty

photographie f photograph

pièce f piece; de monnaie coin

pied m foot

pied de porc m pig's foot

pigeonneau m squab, young pigeon

pigeons aux petits pois See National Dishes p. 30

pignon m pinion

pilule f pill

piment m hot red chili

pincée f a pinch of

Pinot blanc See Wines p. 94

Pinot noir See Wines p. 94

pintade f guinea fowl

pintade flambée aux pommes See National Dishes p. 30

piperade See Regional Dishes p. 39

piquante See Sauces p. 76

piscine f swimming pool

Pissaladière See Regional Dishes p. 54

pissenlit m dandelion

pistache f pistacchio

pithiviers des rois See National Dishes p. 30

place f seat

plaisir m pleasure, fun

plante f plant

plat m dish, plate; **plat principal** main dish or main course

plateau m tray

plein(e) full

plume f feather, pen

plus more

pôcheuse See Regional Dishes p. 42

poêle f frying pan

poids m weight

point (à) See Gastronomic Terms p. 82

poire f pear

Poire belle dijonnaise See Regional Dishes p. 42

Poire belle-Hélène See Recipes p. 62

poires farcies des santons See Regional Dishes p. 55

poireau m leek

pois chiches mpl chickpeas

poisson m fish

poitrine de veau farcie See National Dishes p. 30

poivrade See Sauces p. 76

poivre m pepper

poivre vert m green pepper

poivron m bell pepper

Pomerol See Wines p. 94

pomme f apple

pomme de terre f potato

  pommes Dauphine See Gastronomic Terms p. 85

pommes de terre bouillies boiled potatoes; **pommes de terre frites** French fries; **pommes de terre sautées** fried, sautéed potatoes; **pommes de terre vapeur** steamed potatoes

pont-l'Evêque See Cheeses p. 15

porc m pork

porc rôti aux pommes See National Dishes p. 31 and Recipes p. 62

porte f door

portefeuille m wallet

porter to bring, to carry

Port-Salut See Cheeses p. 15

potable drinkable

potage m soup

potager m vegetable garden

pot-au-feu See National Dishes p. 31

potée See Gastronomic Terms p. 85

potée "au vieux port" See Regional Dishes p. 53

potiron m pumpkin

poudre f powder

Pouilly-Fuissé See Wines p. 94

Pouilly fumé See Wines p. 94

poule f hen, fowl

poule au pot farcie See National Dishes p. 31

poulet m chicken

poulet à la crème See Regional Dishes p. 42

poulet à l'estragon See National Dishes p. 31 and Recipes p. 63

poulet au Maroilles See Regional Dishes p. 52

poulet basquaise See Regional Dishes p. 40 and Recipes p. 64

poulet Marengo See National Dishes p. 31

poulet sauté au Champagne See Regional Dishes p. 45
poulette See Sauces p. 76
Pouligny-Saint-Pierre See Cheeses p. 15
poulpe m octopus
pounti auvergnat See Regional Dishes p. 41
pour for
pourboire m tip
pourquoi why
pousse de soja f bean sprouts
poussette f stroller
pouvoir to be able to
préférer to prefer
prendre to take
prénom m first name, christian name
préparer to prepare
près de near, near to
près close
presque nearly, almost
printemps m spring (season)
prix m price
produit alimentaire m foodstuff
profiteroles au chocolat See National Dishes p. 31
propre own, clean
provençale (à la) See Gastronomic Terms p. 82
Provence-Côte d'Azur Provence-French Riviera

prune f plum
pruneau m prune
pruneaux au Sauternes See Regional Dishes p. 40
puant-macéré See Cheeses p. 15
pulpe f pulp
purée f purée
purée de céleri-rave See National Dishes p. 31
purée de pois cassés See National Dishes p. 32

qu'est-ce-que cela veut dire? What does that mean?
quand when
quart quarter
quartier m quarter, neighborhood
que what
quel which
quelqu'un someone, anyone somebody, anybody
quelque(s) some, a few
quelque chose something,
quenelles See Gastronomic Terms p. 85
questche See Liqueurs p. 19
question f question
queue f line (of people), stem (fruit), tail
qui who, whom
quiche Lorraine See National Dishes p. 32, Regional

Dishes p. 48 and Recipes p. 65
quiconque whoever
quoi what

rabais m discount
râble See Gastronomic Terms p. 85
radis m radish
raffiné(e) refined
ragoût See Gastronomic Terms p. 85
raie au beurre noir See National Dishes p. 32 and Recipes p. 66
raisin m grape
raisins secs mpl raisins
randonnée f hike, drive
râpé(e) grated
rapide rapid
rapidement rapidly
Ratafia See Liqueurs p. 20
ratatouille provençale See Regional Dishes p. 55
ravigote See Sauces p. 76
reblochon See Cheeses p. 16
recette f recipe
réchauffer to warm up
récipient m container
réclamation f complaint
reçu m receipt
réfrigérateur m refrigerator
refroidir to chill, to cool
regarder to look

régime m diet
région f region
règlement m payment **par chèque** by check; **en espèces** in cash
réglisse f liquorice
religieuse See National Dishes p. 32
remboursement m reimbursement
remercier to thank
rémoulade See Sauces p. 76
rencontrer to meet
rendez-vous m appointment
renseignement m information
repas m meal
répondre to answer
réputé(e) renowned
réservation f reservation
réservé(e) reserved
réserver to reserve
rester to remain
retard m delay, **être en retard** to be late
retour m return
Reuilly See Wines p. 95
revenir to come back
rien nothing
Riesling See Wines p. 95
rillettes See Cold Cuts p. 80
rillons See Cold Cuts p. 80
ris de veau en cocotte See National Dishes p. 32

ris de veau Joseph See Regional Dishes p. 46

rissolé(e) browned

riz m rice

riz au lait See National Dishes p. 32

riz gaxuxa See Regional Dishes p. 40

rognon m kidney

rognons de veau à la moutarde See National Dishes p. 32

rollot See Cheeses p. 16

romarin m rosemary

roquefort See Cheeses p. 16

Rosé d'Anjou See Wines p. 95

rosé de Marsannay See Wines p. 95

rosette See Cold Cuts p. 80

rôti roasted; See National Dishes p. 32

rôti de porc à l'orange See National Dishes p. 32

rôti de veau Orloff See National Dishes p. 33

rôti en croûte See National Dishes p. 33

rôtisserie f shop selling roast meat, steakhouse

rouge red

rouget m mullet

rougets en papillotes See National Dishes p. 33

rouille See Sauces p. 76

Roussette de Savoie See Wines p. 95

route f road

rue f street

rumsteak m rumpsteak

rustique rustic

sabayon m zabaglione

sablé(e) sablé pastry, cookie

sac m bag

safran m safran

saignant(e) (cul.) See Gastronomic Terms p. 86

saindoux m lard

Saint-Amour See Wines p. 95

Saint-Chinian See Wines p. 95

Saint-Emilion See Wines p. 95

Saint-Estèphe See Wines p. 95

saint-Honoré See National Dishes p. 33

Saint-Joseph See Wines p. 95

Saint-Julien See Wines p. 96

saint-maure See Cheeses p. 16

saint-nectaire See Cheeses p. 16

saint-paulin See Cheeses p. 16

Saint-Pourçain See Wines p. 95

SAI-SER

Saint-Véran See Wines p. 96
saison f season
salade f salad
salade landaise See Regional Dishes p. 40
salade niçoise See National Dishes p. 33
sale dirty
salé(e) salty
salière f salt shaker
salle f room
salle de bains f bathroom
salmis See Gastronomic Terms p. 86
salmis de palombes See Regional Dishes p. 40
samedi Saturday
Sancerre See Wines p. 96
sang m blood
sans without
sans alcool alcohol-free
sarment du Médoc See Sweets p. 9
sarriette savory
sarrasin m buckwheat
sauce f sauce; **sauce tomate** f tomato sauce
saucisse f sausage; **saucisses de Strasbourg** type of beef sausage
saucisson See Cold Cuts p. 80
saucisson chaud lyonnais See Regional Dishes p. 56

sauf except
sauge f sage
saumon m salmon **saumon fumé** smoked salmon
saupiquet du Morvan See Regional Dishes p. 44
sauté See Gastronomic Terms p. 86
sauté d'agneau à la navarraise See Regional Dishes p. 40
Sauternes See Wines p. 96
savarin See National Dishes p. 33
Savigny-lès-Beaune See Wines p. 96
savoir to know
savon m soap
savoureux(euse) tasty
scarole f escarole
schiffala See Regional Dishes p. 37
sec (sèche) dry
second(e) second
seiche f cuttlefish
seigle m rye
sel m salt
semaine f week
semoule f semolina
sentir to feel
septembre September
serpolet m wild thyme
serveur(euse) waiter/ waitress
service m service charge

service compris service included; **service non compris/s.n.c.** service not included
serviette de table f napkin
servir to serve
seul(e) alone
seulement only
signifier to signify, to mean
simple easy, simple
sirop syrup
socca See Regional Dishes p. 55
soif f thirst
soir m evening
soja m soya
sole f sole (fish)
soles au Champagne See Regional Dishes p. 46
sommelier m wine waiter
sorbet sherbet; See National Dishes p. 33
sortie f exit
sortir to exit, to go out
soubise See Sauces p. 76
soufflé au fromage See National Dishes p. 33 and Recipes p. 66
soufflé au Roquefort See Regional Dishes p. 49
soupe f soup
soupe aux huîtres See Regional Dishes p. 43 and National Dishes p. 34

soupe à l'oignon See National Dishes p. 33 and Recipes p. 67
soupe au chou See National Dishes p. 34
soupe de poissons See National Dishes p. 34
soupe des Hortillons See Regional Dishes p. 53
souper m dinner
sous under
souvent often
spectacle m show
steak au poivre vert See National Dishes p. 34
steak de lotte au poivre vert See Regional Dishes p.
steak/frites See National Dishes p. 34
steak grillé m grilled steak
sucré(e) sweetened
sucre m sugar **en morceaux** sugar cubes; **en poudre** granulated; **glace** icing sugar, powdered sugar
sucrier m sugar bowl
sud south
suffire to suffice, to be enough
Suisse Switzerland
supermarché m supermarket
supplément m supplement
suprême See Sauces p. 76
sur on

sûr(e) sure
surgelé(e) frozen
Sylvaner See Wines p. 96

table f table
tablette de chocolat f bar of chocolate
talc m talcum powder
tard late
tarif m rate, price
tartare See Sauces p. 76
tarte f pie
tarte au citron See National Dishes p. 34
tarte au Roquefort See National Dishes p. 34 and Recipes p. 68
tarte aux oignons See National Dishes p. 34
tarte Ervalenta See Regional Dishes p. 41
tarte flambée au Calvados See Regional Dishes p. 51
tarte tante Catherine See Regional Dishes p. 45
tarte Tatin See National Dishes p. 34 and Recipes p. 69
tartelette f tart
tartine f slice of bread with butter/jam
tasse f cup
Tavel See Wines p. 96
taxe f tax; **toutes taxes**

comprises (T.T.C.) inclusive of taxes
téléphone m telephone
température f temperature
temps m weather, time
tendre tender
tête de veau f calf's head
terminus m terminus
terrasse f terrace
terrine See Gastronomic Terms p. 86
terrine de foies de volaille See National Dishes p. 35
terrine de saumon See National Dishes p. 35
tétine f teat
thé m tea **thé au citron** tea with lemon; **thé nature** tea without milk
théière f teapot
thon m tuna
thym m thyme
tiède lukewarm
tilleul m lime (tree)
timbale f tumbler, mold
timbre m stamp
tire-bouchon m corkscrew
tisane f herbal tea
Tokay Pinot Gris See Wines p. 96
tomate f tomato
tomates à la provençale See National Dishes p. 35 and Recipes p. 70

tomates farcies See stuffed tomatoes p. 35
tomber to fall
tomme de Savoie See Cheeses p. 17
tôt soon, early
toujours always
tour m stroll, walk, drive
Touraine See Wines p. 97
tournedos m round beef fillet
tournedos au poivre vert See Regional Dishes p. 49
tournedos Rossini See National Dishes p. 35 and Recipes p. 71
tourner to turn, to rotate
tourons See Regional Dishes p. 40
tourte Augeronne au Livarot et au Pont l'Evèque See Regional Dishes p. 51
tourte gasconne See Regional Dishes p. 40
tourte quercynnoise See Regional Dishes p. 49
tout all
toux f cough
train m train
traiteur m caterer and delicatessen
tranche f slice
transport m transportation
travail m work
tripes f tripe

trop too much, too many
trouver to find
truffe f truffle; **truffe blanche** white truffle; **truffe noire** black truffle
truite f trout
truite au bleu See Regional Dishes p. 37
truite aux amandes See National Dishes p. 35 and Recipes p. 72
truites aux laitue See Regional Dishes p. 41
truites farcies Luxueil See Regional Dishes p. 46
truites Nano See Regional Dishes p. 49
T.T.C. See **taxe**
tuiles aux amandes See Sweets p. 9
turbot m flounder (fish)
TVA VAT

urgence f emergency
user to use
utiliser to use, to adopt

vacances fpl vacation holidays
vacherin des Bauges See Cheeses p. 17
valençay See Cheeses p. 17
valise f suitcase
valois See Sauces p. 76

vanille f vanilla
vapeur steam; **à la vapeur** steamed
veau m calf, veal
végétal(e) vegetable
végétarien See Gastronomic Terms p. 86
velouté m cream soup
vendange f grape harvest
vendeu(r)(euse) salesman, saleswoman
vendôme bleu See Cheeses p. 17
vendre to sell
vendredi Friday
venir to come
verre m glass; **verre de contact** contact lenses
vers towards
versement m deposit
vert(e) green; See Sauces p. 77
verveine f verbena tea
veste f jacket
vestiaire m cloakroom
vêtement m garment
vétérinaire m veterinarian
viande f meat; **hachée** minced, ground
vide empty
vieux, vieille old
vigne f vine

ville f city
vin m wine; **blanc** white wine; **rosé** rosé wine; **rouge** red wine
Vin de paille See Wines p. 97
Vin de pays See Wines p. 97
Vin jaune See Wines p. 97
vinaigre m vinegar; **de vin** wine vinegar
vinaigrette See Sauces p. 77
vitamine f vitamin
vite fast
voir to see
vol m flight
vouloir to want
Vouvray See Wines p. 97
voyage m trip
vue f sight, view

wagon m wagon
Williamine See Liqueurs p. 20

yaourt m yoghurt
yeux mpl eyes

zikiro See Regional Dishes p. 41
zut ! (expression) "Darn it !"

able to, to be pouvoir *poov-wahr*

above dessus *duh-soo*

according to d'après *dah-preh*

account l'addition *lah-dee-see-ohn*

ache mal *mahl*

acid aigre *ay-gruh*

additive additif *ah-dee-teef*

address adresse *ahd-drehs*

adult adulte *ah-doolt*

after après *ah-preh*

afterwards ensuite **ahn-soo-weet**

against contre *kohn-truh*

age âge *ahj*

ahead avant *ah-vahn*

air air *ayr*

air conditioning climatisation *clee- mah-tee-za-see-ohn*

airplane avion *ah-vee-ohn*

airport aéroport *ah-ay-roh-pohr*

à la carte *ah-lah-kahrt*

a lot beaucoup *boh-coo*

alcoholic alcoolique *ahl-kool-ee-kuh*

alcoholic drinks boissons alcoolisées *boo-wah-sohn al-kool- ee-zay*

alert alerte *ah-lehrt*

all tout *too*

allergy allergie *ahl-lerh-jee*

allowed permis *pehr-mee*

almonds amandes *ah-mahnd*

almost presque *prehs-kuh*

also aussi *oh-see*

always toujours *too-joor*

American coffee café allongé *kah-feh ah-lohn-jay*

among(st) parmi *pahr-mee*

anchovy anchois *ahn-shwah*

angle angle *ahn-gluh*

angling pêcher *peh-shay*

anise anis *ah-nees*

announcement annonce *ah-nohs*

answer, to répondre *ray-pohn-druh*

antibiotic antibiotique *ahn-tee-bee-oh-teek*

any n'importe quel *nehm-pohrt kehl*

anybody n'importe qui *nehm-pohrt kee*

anything n'importe quoi *nehm-pohrt koo-wah*

aperitif apéritif *ah-peh-ree-teef*

appetite *ah-peh-tee* **enjoy your meal** Bon appétit ! *bohn ah-peh-tee*

appetizers amuse-gueule *ah-mooz-gehl*

apple pomme *puhm*

application (job) demande *deh-mahnd*

appointment rendez-vous rahn-day-_voo_

apricot abricot ah-bree-_koh_

April avril ah-_vreel_

aroma/fragrances arôme ah-_rohm_/ parfums pahr-_faym_

aromatic aromatique ah-roh-mah-_teek_

arrive, to arriver ah-ree-_vay_

artichoke artichaut ahr-tee-_shoh_

as comme kahm

as far as jusqu'à _joos_-kah

as well aussi oh-_see_

ash(es) cendres _sahn_-druh

ashtray cendrier sahn-dree-_ay_

ask, to demander deh-mahn-_day_

asparagus asperges ahs-_pehr_-juh

aspirin aspirine ahs-pee-_reen_

at least au moins oh-moo-_ayn_

attentive prevenant preh-veh-_nahn_

August août oot

Austria Autriche oh-_tree_-shuh

authentic authentique oh-tahn-_teek_

avocado avocat ah-voh-_kah_

avoid, to éviter ay-vee-_tay_

awkward peu commode peh koh-_mohd_

back derrière deh-ree-_ayr_

backwards en arrière ahn ah-ree-_ayr_

bacon lard lahr

bad mauvais(e) moh-_veh(z)_

bag sac sahk

baking cuisson (au four) coo-wee-_sohn_ oh foor

banana banane bah-_nahn_

bank banque bahnk

bar bistrot bees-_troh_

barley orge ohrj

basil basilic bah-zee-_leek_

bass (fish) bar bahr

bath bain bayn

Bavarian Bavarois(e) Bah-vahr-_wah(z)_

bay laurier loh-ree-_ay_

be careful attention ah-tahn-see-_ohn_

be enough, to assez ah-_say_

be left, to rester rehs-tay

be sufficient, to suffire soo-feer

beans haricots ah-ree-_koh_

beat, to battre _bah_-truh

beautiful belle behl

because parce que _pahr_-seh-keh

beef bœuf buhf

beer bière bee-_ayr_

beet/beetroot betterave beh-_trahv_

behind derrière deh-ree-ayr

bell pepper poivron *poo-wah-vrohn*

below au-dessous *oh-dehs-soo*

berry baies *bay*

beside à côté *ah-koh-tay*

best meilleur(e) *may-yehr*

better meilleur/mieux *may-yehr/mee-yuh*

between entre *ahn-truh*

big grand(e) *grahn(d)*

bill l'addition *lah-dee-see-ohn*

biscuits petit gâteaux secs *peh-tee gah-toh sehk*

bitter âpre *ah-pruh*

bitter liqueur liqueur amère *lee-kehr ah-mayr*

bittersweet aigre-doux *ay-gruh-doo*

black noir(e) *noo-wahr*

blackcurrant cassis *kah-sees*

blend mélange *meh-lahnj*

blouse corsage *kohr-sahj*

boil, to bouillir *boo-yeer*

boiled eggs oeufs durs *ehf-door*

boiling bouillant(e) *boo-yahn(t)*

bone os *ohs*

book livre *lee-vruh*

bottle bouteille *boo-tay-ee-yuh*

bottled embouteillé *ahm-boo-tay-ee-yay*

bottle-opener ouvre-bouteille *oo-vruh boo-tay-ee-yuh*

bovine bovin *boh-vayn*

box boîte *boo-waht*

boy garçon *gahr-sohn*

brain cerveau *sehr-voh*

braised braisé(e) *bray-zay*

brandy cognac *kohn-yahk*

bread pain *payn*

breadcrumbs chapelure *shah-peh-loor*

break, to casser *kahs-say*

breakfast petit déjeuner *peh-tee day-jeh-nay*

bream brème *brehm*

breast poitrine *pwah-treen*

bring, to apporter *ah-pohr-tay*

broadbeans fève *fehv*

broken cassé(e) *kahs-say*

browned doré *doh-ray*

brush brosse *brohs*

Brussel sprouts choux de bruxelles *shoo-deh- broo-xehl*

buds bourgeons *boor-gee-ohn*

burn, to brûler *broo-lay*

burnt brûlé(e) *broo-lay*

busy occupé(e) *oh-koo-pay*

but mais *may*

butcher's boucherie *boo-sheh-ree*

butter beurre *behr*
buttered beurré *behr-ray*
button bouton *boo-tohn*
buy, to acheter *ah-sheh-tay*
by way of via *vee-ah*

cabbage chou *shoo*
cake gâteau *gah-toh*
cake shop pâtisserie *pah-tee-seh-ree*
calf veau *voh*
call, to appeler *ah-play*
calm calme *kahlm*
calming calmant *kahl-mahn*
camomile camomille *kah-moh-mee-yuh*
campaign campagne *kahm-pahn-yuh*
can pouvoir *poov-wahr*
to cancel annuler *ah-nyoo-lay*
candied confit(e), *kohn-fee(t)*, glacé *glah-say*
candle bougie *boo-jee*
candy bonbon *bohn-bohn*
capers câpres *kah-pruh*
capon chapon *sha-pohn*
car voiture *voo-wah-toor*
carafe *kah-rahf*
caramel *kah-rah-mehl*
caretaker gardien(ne) *gahr-dee-ayn(nuh)*
carrot carotte *kah-roht*
carry, to porter *pohr-tay*

cash espèces *ehs-pehs*
cash desk caisse *kehs*
cashier cassier *keh-see-ay*
cauliflower chou-fleur *shoo-flehr*
caviar *kah-vee-ahr*
celery céleri *seh-leh-ree*
cellar cave, *kahv*
central central(e) *sehn-trahl*
cereals céréales *say-ray-ahl*
chair chaise *shayz*
change, to changer *shan-jay*
chard bette *beht*
charge, to débiter *day-bee-tay*
cheap bon marché *bohn-mahr-shay*
check, to contrôler *kohn-troh-lay*
check-out caisse *kehs*
cheese fromage *froh-maj*
chemist's pharmacie *fahr-mah-see*
cheque/check chèque *shehk*
cherry cerise *say-reez*
chest poitrine *poo-wah-treen*
chestnuts châtaigne *shah-tehn-yuh* marrons *mahr-rohn*
chew, to mastiquer *mahs-tee-kay*
chick peas pois chiche *poo-wah sheesh*

chicken poulet *poo-lay*
chicken leg/thigh (drumstick) cuisse de poulet *koo-wees duh poo-lay*
chicory chicorée *shee-koh-ray*
child enfant *ahn-fahn*
chili pepper piment rouge *pee-mahn rooj*
chocolate chocolat *shoh-koh-lah*
chocolates chocolats *shoh-koh-lah*
chop, to couper, *koo-pay* hâcher *ah-shay*
chopped hâchée *ah-shay*
Christmas Noel *noh-ehl*
cigar cigare *see-gahr*
cinnamon cannelle *kah-nehl*
citron cédrat *say-drah*
citrus fruit agrumes *ah-groom*
city ville *veel*
clams praires *prehr*
clean propre *proh-pruh*
clear clair(e) *klayr*
client(e) klee-*ahn(t)*
cloakroom vestiaire *vehs-tee-ayr*
close, to fermer *fehr-may*
closed fermé *fehr-may*
closure fermeture *fehr-meh-toor*
coat manteau *mahn-toh*

cockerel jeune coq *juhn kahk*
cocoa cacao *kah-kah-oh*
coconut noix de coco *noo-wah duh koh-koh*
cod morue *moo-roo*
coffee café *kahf-fay*
coffee with a dash of milk café au lait *kahf-fay oh-lay*
coin pièce de monnaie *pee-ehs duh mohn-nay*
cold froid(e) *froo-wah(d)*
color couleur *koo-lehr*
come, to venir *veh-neer*
comfortable confortable *kohn-fohr-tah-bluh*
company société *soh-see-ay-tay*
complaint plainte *playnt*
complete complet(ète) *kohm-pleh(t)*
compulsory obligatoire *oh-blee-gah-too-wahr*
conclusion fin *fayn*
cone (ice-cream) cornet *kohr-nay*
confirm, to confirmer *kohn-feer-may*
contact lenses verres de contact *vehr-duh- kohn-tah*
continue, to continuer *kohn-tee-noo-ay*
control, to contrôler *kohn-troh-lay*

convenient commode *kohm-mohd*

cook, to cuisiner *kwee-zee-nay*

cooked cuit(e) *koo-wee(t)*

cooking cuisine *kwee-zeen*

cool frais(che) *fray, fraysh*

to cool refroidir *reh-froo-wah-deer*

corn mais *mah-ees*

corner coin *koo-wayn*

cost coût *koo*

cost, to coûter *koo-tay*

cotton coton *koh-tohn*

country pays *pah-ee*

countryside campagne *kahm-pahn-yuh*

course plat *plah*

cover, to couvrir *koo-vreer*

crab crabe *krahb*

cranberries canneberges *kahn-behrj*

crayfish langoustine *lahn-goo-steen*

cream crème *krehm*

creampuff choux à la crème *shoo-ah-lah krehm*

credit card carte de crédit *kahrt duh kray-dee*

crisp croquant(e) *kroh-kahn(t)*

crowded plein(e) *pleh(n)*

cucumber concombre *kohn-kohm-bruh*

cummin cumin *kee-yoo-mayn*

cup tasse *tahs*

currency monnaie *mohn-nay*

cushion cousin *koo-sayn*

customer client(e) *klee-yahn(t)*

cut, to couper *koo-pay*

cutlery couverts *koo-vehr*

cutlet côtelette *koh-teh-leht*

cuttlefish seche *seh-shuh*

dance, to danser *dahn-say*

date rendez-vous *rahn-day-voo*

dates (fruit) dattes *daht*

daughter fille *fee-yuh*

day jour *joor*

dear cher(ère) *shehr*

debit, to débiter *day-bee-tay*

decaffeinated décaféiné(e) day- *kah-fee-ee-nay*

decanter carafe *kah-rahf*

December décembre *day-sahm-bruh*

decorated decoré(e) *deh-koh-ray*

delay retard *reh-tahr*

dentures dentier *dahn-tee-ay*

deposit, to déposer *day-poh-zay*

dessert dessert *deh-sehr*

diabetic diabétique *dee-ah-bay-teek*

diet régime *ray-jeem*
different différent *dee-fay-rahn*
difficult difficile *dee-fee-seel*
digestible digeste *dee-gehst*
digestive digestif *dee-gehs-teef*
dinner dîner *dee-nay*
directions indications *ayn-dee-kah-see-ohn*
director directeur *dee-rehk-tehr*
directory annuaire *ahn-noo-wayr*
dirty sale *sahl*
disabled handicapé *ahn-dee-kahp-pay*
disinfect, to désinfecter *dayz-ayn-fehk-tay*
disinfectant désinfectant *dehz- ayn-fehk-tahn*
distributor distributeur *dehs-tree-boo-tehr*
disturb, to déranger *deh-rahn-jay*
do, to faire *fehr*
doctor (medecin) médecin *may-deh- sayn*
door porte *pohrt*
dough pâte *paht*
doughnut beignet *behn-yay*
down /downstairs en bas *ahn bah*

draught beer bière à la pression *bee-ehr ah lah preh-see-ohn*
dressing assaisonnement *ah-say-zohn-mahn*
digestible digeste *dee-gehst*
dried/dry sec *sehk*
dried fruit fruits secs *froo-ee sehk*
dried mushrooms champignons secs *sham-pee-yohn sehk*
drink boisson *boo-wah-sohn*
drink, to boire *boo-wahr*
duck canard *kah-nahr*
Dutch hollandais(e) *oh-lahn-dehz*

each chaque *shahk*
earring boucle d'oreille *boo-cluh doh-ray-ee-yuh*
Easter Pâques *pahk*
easy facile *fah-seel*
eat, to manger *mahn-jay*
economical economique *ay-koh-noh-meek*
E.E.C. (European Economic Community) CEE *say-ay-ay eel anguille ahn-gee-yuh*
egg œuf *ehf*
egg white blanc d'œuf *blahn dehf*
eggs fried in butter œufs frits dans le beurre *eh free dahn luh behr*

191

elevator ascenseur *ah-sahn-sehr*

embassy ambassade *ahm-bah-sahd*

empty vide *veed*

enclosed clôturé(e) *kloh-too-ray*

end fin *fayn*

engaged occupé(e) *oh-koo-pay*

England Angleterre *ahn-gleh-tehr*

English anglais(e) *ahn-glay(z)*

enjoyment plaisir *play-zeer*

enough assez *ah-say*

enter, to entrer *ahn-tray*

entrance/entry entrée *ahn-tray*

envelope enveloppe *ahn-veh-lohp*

equal égale *ay-gahl*

error erreur *eh-rehr*

etiquette étiquette *ay-tee-keht*

evening soir *soo-wahr*

ever jamais *jah-may*

every chaque *shahk*

everything tout *too*

evil mauvais(e) *moh-veh(z)*

except sauf *sahf*

exchange change *shanj*

exit sortie *sohr-tee*

expense dépense *day-pahns*

expensive cher(ère) *shehr*

experienced expérimenté(e) *ehks- peh-ree-mahn-tay*

express (café express) *ehks-prehs*

external extérieur *eks-teh-ray-ehr*

extract extrait *ehks-tray*

eye œil *oo-yuh/* pl **eyes** yeux *yuh*

failure échec *ay-shehk*

fainted évanoui(e) *ay-vahn-noo-ee*

fall, to tomber *tohm-bay*

familiar familier(e) *fah-mee-lee-ay, fah-mee-lee-ayr*

family famille *fah-mee-yuh*

famous fameux *fahm-eh*

célèbre *seh-leh-bruh*

far loin *loo-ayn*

fast vite *veet*

fat gros(se) *groh(s)*

favor faveur *fah-vehr*

February février *feh-vree-ay*

feeding alimentation *ah-lee-mehn-tah-see-ohn*

feel, to sentir *sahn-teer*

fennel fenouil *feh-noo-yuh*

few (a) peu *peh*

fig figue *fee-guh*

filled (stuffed) farci(e) *fahr-see*

fillet filet *fee-leh*

filter, to filtrer *feel-tray*

find, to trouver *troo-vay*
fine fin(e) *fayn, feen*
finish, to finire *fee-neer*
fire feu *feh*
first premier(ère) *preh-mee-ay, preh-mee-ehr*
fish poisson *poo-wah-sohn*
fish soup soupe de poisson *soop duh poo-wah-sohn*
fishing pêche *pehsh*
fizzy pétillant(e) *pay-tee-yahn(t)*
flame flamme *flahm*
flat plat(e) *plah(t)*
flavor goût *goo*
flavor, to assaisonner *ah-say-soh-nay*
flavoring parfum *pahr-faym*
flight vol *vohl*
floor étage *ay-tahj*
flour farine *fah-reen*
flower fleur *flehr*
fly mouche *moosh*
food dyes colorants *kohl-ohr-ahn*
food poisoning intoxication alimentaire *ayn-tohks-ee-kah-see-ohn ah-lee-mahn-tayr*
foot pied *pee-ay*
for pour *poor*
foreign étranger(ère) *ay-trahn-jay, ay-trahn-jehr*
forget, to oublier *oo-blee-ay*

fork fourchette *foor-sheht*
forward en avant *ahn ah-vahn*
France France *frahns*
frankfurter saucisse de Francfort *soh-sees duh frahn-fohr*
free gratuit *grah-too-ee*
French français(e) *frahn-say, frahn-sehz*
fresh frais, fraîche *fray, frehsh*
fresh fruit, fruits frais *froo-ee fray*
fresh mushrooms champignon frais *sham-peen-yohn fray*
Friday vendredi *vahn-dreh-dee*
fried frit(e) *free, freet*
friend ami(e) *ah-mee*
fritters beignets *behn-yay*
frozen congelé(e) *kohn-jeh-lay*
fruit fruit *froo-ee*
fruit salad salade de fruits *sah-lahd duh froo-ee*
fruits of the forest fruits de bois *froo-ee duh boo-wah*
frying pan poêle *poo-wahl*
full plein(e) *playn, plehn*
full-bodied qui a du corps *kee ah doo kohr*

game gibier *gee-bee-ay*

garden jardin *jahr-dayn*
garlic ail *ah-yee*
garnishing garnissage *gahr-nee-sahj*
gender genre *jahn*, sexe *sehks*
gentleman monsieur *mehs-yehr*
German allemand(e) *ahl-mahn(d)*
Germany Allemagne *ahl-mahn-yuh*
get, to obtenir *ohb-teh-neer*
gherkin (pickle) cornichon *kohr-nee-shohn*
ginger gingembre *gayn-jahm-bruh*
girl fille *fee-yuh*
give, to donner *dehn-nay*
glass verre *vehr*
gloves gants *gahn*
go, to aller *ah-lay*
gold or *ohr*
golden brown doré *doh-ray*
good bien *bee-ehn*
goose oie *oo-wah*
go out/come out sortir *sohr-teer*
grain grain *grayn*
grapefruit pamplemousse *pahm-pleh-moos*
grapes raisins *ray-sayn*
grated rapé *rah-pay*
greasy gras(se) *grah(s)*

great grand(e) *grahn(d)*
Great Britain Grande Bretagne *grahnd breh-tahn-yuh*
Greece Grèce *grehs*
Greek grec *grehk*
green vert(e) *vehr(t)*
grey mullet mulet *moo-lay*
grill gril *gree-yuh*
grilled steak bifteck grillé *behf-tehk gree-yay*
group groupe *groop*
group leader chef de groupe *shef duh groop*
grouper mérou *may-roo*
guard, to garder *gahr-day*
guide/guidebook guide *geed*
guinea fowl pintade *payn-tahd*

hake colin *kohl-ayn*
half moitié *moo-wah-tee-yay*
hall couloir *kool-wahr*
ham jambon *jahm-bohn*
hand main *mayn*
handbag sac à main *sahk-ah-mayn*
handkerchief mouchoir *moosh-wahr*
happen, to se passer *suh pah-say*
happy content(e) *kohn-tahn(t)*
hard dur(e) *door*
hare lièvre *lee-ehv-ruh*

harmless inoffensif(ve) *ayn-ohf-ahn-seef, ayn-ohf-ahn-seev*

harsh dur(e) *door*, rude *rood*

hat chapeau *shah-poh*

have, to avoir *ahv-wahr*

hazelnuts noisettes *noo-ohee-seht*

headache mal de tête *mahl-duh-teht*

hear, to entendre *ahn-tahn-druh*

heating chauffage *shoh-fahj*

heavy lourd(e) *loor(d)*

help, to aider *ay-day*

helping portion *pohr-see-ohn*

hen poule *pool*

herbs herbes *ehrb*

here ici *ee-see*

herring hareng *ah-rahn*

high chair chaise haute *shehz oht*

high-proof spirits eau-de-vie *oh-duh- vee*

hold, to tenir *teh-neer*

holiday fête *feht*

holidays vacances *vah-kahns*

Holland Hollande *oh-lahnd*

honey miel *mee-ehl*

honey mushrooms armillaire *ahr-mee-yehr*

hospital hôpital *oh-pee-tahl*

hot chaud(e) *shoh(d)*

hotel hôtel *oh-tehl*

hour heure *ehr-ruh*

how comment *koh-mahn*

how much/many combien *kohm-bee-ayn*

hundred cent *sahn*

hunger faim *faym*

hurry hâte *aht*

husband mari *mah-ree*

ice/ice-cream glace *glahs*

ice-cream shop café-glacier *kah-fay glah-see-ay*

ice-cube glaçon *glah-sohn*

icing glaçage *glah-sahj*

identity card carte d'identité *kahrt-dee- dahn-tee-tay*

ill malade *mah-lahd*

immediately tout de suite *toot-duh-soo-eet*

important important(e) *aym-pohr-tahn(t)*

in dans *dahn*

in cash comptant *kohn-tahn*

in order that afin que *ah-fayn-keh*

in order to pour *poor*

included/inclusive inclus(e), *ayn-kloo(z)*

indoors à l'intérieur *ah-l-ayn-tay-ree-ehr*

inexpensive pas cher(ère) *pah shehr*

inform, to informer *ayn-fohr-may*

infusion infusion *ayn-foo-see-ohn*
inn auberge *oh-behrj*
insect insecte *ayn-sehkt*
inside dedans *deh-dahn*
instead au lieu de *oh-lee-yuh-duh*
invite, to inviter *ayn-vee-tay*
invoice facture *fahk-toor*
Ireland Irlande *eer-lahnd*
Italian italien(ne) *ee-tah-lee-yayn ee-tah-lee-yehn*

jacket veston *vehs-tohn*
jam confiture *kohn-fee-toor*
jam tart tartelette à la confiture *tahr-teh-leht ah lah kohn-fee-toor*
January janvier *jahn-vee-ay*
jelly gelée *jeh-lay*
job emploi *ahm-plwah*
jug pot *poh*
juice jus *joo*
July juillet *joo-wee-yay*
June juin *joo-ayn*
juniper genièvre *geh-nee-eh-vruh*
just seulement *suhl-mahn*

keep, to garder *gahr-day*
keeper gardien(ne) *gahr-dee-ayn, gahr-dee-ehn*
khaki kaki *kah-kee*

kid (gloves) chevreau *sheh-vroh*
kidney (food) rognons *rohn-yohn*
kind (type) genre *jahn-ruh*
kitchen cuisine *kwee-zeen*
knife couteau *koo-toh*
know, to savoir *sahv-wahr*

label étiquette *ay-tee-keht*
lady dame *dahm*
lager bière blonde *bee-ayr blohnd*
lake lac *lahk*
lamb agneau *ahn-yoh*
land terre *tehr*
lard saindoux *sayn-doo*
large grand(e) *grahn(d)*
last dernier(ère) *dehr-nee-ay, dehr-nee-ayr*
laugh rire *reer*
lean maigre *may-gruh*
leave, to quitter *kee-tay*
leek poireau *poo-wah-roh*
leg jambe *jahmb*
lemon citron *see-trohn*
lemonade jus de citron pressé *joo-duh-see-trohn preh-say*
lentils lentilles *lahn-tee-yuh*
less moins *moo-wayn*
let, to (to permit) laisser *leh-say*
let go of, to lâcher *lah-shay*

lettuce laitue *lay-too*
lift (elevator) ascenseur *ah-sahn-sehr*
light (weight) leger(ère) *leh-jay, leh-jehr*
like, to aimer (bien) *ay-may (bee-ehn)*
line ligne *leen-yuh*
liqueur glass verre à liqueur *vehr ah lee-kehr*
list liste *leest*
little petit(e) *peh-tee(t)*
liver foie *foo-wah*
lobster homard *oh-mahr*
loin (beef) aloyau *ah-loh-yoh*
long long(ue) *lohn, lohn(guh)*
lose, to perdre *pehr-druh*
loud (noise) fort(e) *fohr(t)*
lovely joli(e) *joh-lee*
lunch déjeuner *day-jeh-nay*
mackerel maquereau *mah-kroh*
macrobiotic macrobiotique *mah-kroh-bee-oh-teek*
maize maïs *mah-ees*
make, to faire *fehr*
management direction *dee-rehk-see-ohn*
mandarin mandarine *mahn-dah-reen*
manner manière *mah-nee-ehr*
map carte *kahrt*
March mars *mahrs*

marinate, to mariner *mah-ree-nay*
market marché *mahr-shay*
marmalade confiture *kohn-fee-toor*
marrow (bone) moelle *moo-wahl*
match allumette *ah-loo-meht*
mature mûr *moor*
May mai *may*
meal repas *reh-pah*
meaning signification *seen-yee-fee-kah-see-ohn*
means moyens *moh-yehn*
meat viande *vee-ahnd*
meatballs boulettes de viande *boo-leht duh vee-ahnd*
medicine médecine *mayd-seen*
meet, to rencontrer *rahn-kohn-tray*
middle au milieu *oh meel-yeh*
milk lait *lay*
mince, to hâcher *ah-shay*
minced hâché(e) *ah-shay*
mineral water eau minérale *oh mee-nay-rahl*
mint menthe *mahnt*
minus moins *moo-wayn*
Miss mademoiselle *mahd-moo-wah-zehl*
mistake erreur *ehr-rehr*

misunderstanding malentendu *mahl-ahn-tahn-doo*

mix mélange *may-lahnj*

molluscs mollusques *moh-loosk*

Monday lundi *lehn-dee*

month mois *moo-wah*

more plus *ploo*

morning matin *mah-tayn*

mosquitoes moustiques *moos-teek*

most la plupart (de) *lah ploo-pahr*

mother mère *mehr*

mouth bouche *boosh*

much beaucoup *boh-koo*

mullet mulet *moo-leh*

museum musée *moo-say*

mushrooms champignons *sham-peen-yohn*

music musique *moo-seek*

mussels moules *mool*

must devoir *dehv-wahr*

mustard moutarde *moo-tahrd*

mutton mouton *moo-tohn*

name nom *nohm*

napkin serviette *sehr-vee-eht*

narrow étroit(e) *ay-trwah(t)*

nearby proche *prohsh*

nearly presque *prehsk*

need avoir besoin de *ahv-wahr buhz-wayn duh*

never jamais *jah-may*

newspaper journal *joor-nahl*

New Year's Day jour de l'an *joor duh lahn*

no (none) aucun(e) *oh-kahn, au-koon*

nobody personne *pehr-sohn*

noise bruit *broo-wee*

noisy bruyant(e) *broo-yahn(t)*

non-alcoholic non alcoolisée *nohn ahl-koo-lee-zay*

non-smoker non-fumeur *nohn foo-mehr*

none aucun(e) *oh-kahn, oh-koon*

noodles nouilles, *noo-yuh,* pâtes *paht*

north nord *nohr*

not much pas beaucoup *pah boh-koo*

nothing rien *ree-ehn*

nourishment alimentation *ah-lee-mehn-tah-see-ohn*

November novembre *noh-vahm-bruh*

now maintenant *mayn-teh-nahn*

number nombre *nohm-bruh*

nutcracker casse-noix *kahs-noo-wah*

nutmeg muscade *moos-kahd*

oats avoine *ah-voo-wahn*

obligatory obligatoire *oh-blee-gah-twahr*
obtain, to obtenir *ohb-teh-neer*
October octobre *ohk-toh-bruh*
odor odeur *oh-dehr*
offal abats *ah-bah*
often souvent *soo-vahn*
oil huile *oo-weel*
oily huileux(se) *oo-wee-luh(z)*
old vieux, vielle *vee-yuh, vee-ay-yuh*
olives olives *oh-leev*
on sur *soor*
on foot à pied *ah pee-ay*
on top en haut *ahn oh*
onion oignon *ohn-yohn*
only seulement *sehl-mahn*
open/open air ouvert, *oo-vehr,* plein air *playn-ayr*
opposite (across) en face *ahn fahs*
orange *oh-ranj*
orange soda orangeade *oh-rahnj-ahd*
order (restaurant) commande *koh-mahnd*
oregano origan *oh-ree-gahn*
original original(e) *oh-ree-jee-nahl*
other autre *oh-truh*
out of order en panne *ahn pahn*
outfit tenue *teh-noo*

outside dehors *deh-ohr*
oven four *foor*
over dessus *dehs-soo*
overseas outre-mer *oo-truh-mehr*
own propre *proh-pruh*
ox bœuf *buh*
oysters huîtres *oo-wee-truh*

packet colis *koh-lee*
pain douleur *doo-lehr*
pair paire *payr*
pale pâle *pahl*
park parc *pahrk*
parsley persil *pehr-see*
part partie *pahr-tee*
party fête *feht*
passport passeport *pahs-pohr*
pasta pâtes *paht*
pastry pâtisserie *pah-tee-sehr-ee*
pay, to payer *pay-yay*
payment paiement *pay-mahn*
peach pêche *pehsh*
peanut cacahuète *kah-koo-weht*
pear poire *poo-wahr*
peas pois *poo-wah*
pencil crayon *kray-ohn*
pepper poivre *poo-wah-vruh*
pepper-mill moulin à poivre *moo-layn ah poo-wah-vruh*
per par *pahr*
perch (fish) perche *pehrsh*

perhaps peut-être *peh-teh-truh*
permit permis *pehr-mee*
pheasant faisan *fay-sahn*
photograph photo *foh-toh*
pickles cornichons *koh-nee-shohn*
pie tarte *tahrt*
piece morceau *mohr-soh*
pig cochon *koh-shohn*
pike brochet *broh-shey*
pill pilule *pee-lool*
pillow oreiller *oh-ray-yay*
pineapple ananas *ah-nah-nas*
pistachio nuts pistache *pees-tahsh*
place/cover charge couvert *koo-vehr*
place lieu *lee-yuh*
plan plan *plahn*
plaster/band aid pansement *pahns-mahn* adhésif *ahd-hay-zeef*
plate assiette *ah-see-yeht*
play, to jouer *joo-ay*
please s'il vous plaît *seel-voo-play*
pleasure plaisir *play-zeer*
plums prunes *proon*
point out, to signaler *seen-yah-lay*
popsicle glace sur un bâtonnet *glahs soor ahn bah-toh-nay*

pork porc *pohr*
pork meats viandes de porc *vee-ahnd duh pohr*
postcard carte postale *kahrt pohs-tahl*
pot casserole *kahs-seh-rohl*
potatoes pommes de terre *pohm-duh-tehr*
pounded (meat) haché *ah-shay*
power (electricity) courant *koo-rahn*
pram landau *lahn-doh*
prawns crevettes roses *kruh-veht rohz*
prefer, to préférer *pray-fay-ray*
pregnant enceinte *ahn-saynt*
prepare, to préparer *pray-pah-ray*
prescription ordonnance *ohr-doh-nahs*
preservatives conservateurs *kohn-sehr-vah-tehr*
preserved conservé *kohn-sehr-vay*
price prix *pree*
puff pastry pâte feuilletée *paht feh-yuh-tay*
pulp pulpe *poolp*
pumpkin potiron *poh-tee-rohn*
purpose but *boot*
put mettre *meht-truh*

quail caille _kah-yuh_
quarter quart _kahr_
question demande _duh-mahnd_
quick rapide _rah-peed_
quickly rapidement _rah-peed-mahn_
quietly silencieusement _see-lahn-see-ehz-mahn_

rabbit lapin _lah-payn_
radishes radis _rah-dee_
raincoat imperméable _aym-pehr-may-ah-bluh_
raisins raisin sec _ray-sayn sehk_
raspberries framboises _frahm-bwahz_
raw cru(e) _kroo_
read, to lire _leer_
ready prêt(e) _preh(t)_
ready-made tout fait _too fay_
really vraiment _vray-mahn_
receipt reçu _reh-soo_
red rouge _rooj_
refrigerator réfrigérateur _ray-free-jay-rah-tehr,_
refund remboursement _rahm-boors-mahn_
region région _ray-jee-ohn_
remain, to rester _rehs-tay_
remainder le reste _luh rehst_
remove, to enlever _ahn-leh-vay_

rent louer _loo-way_
reply, to répondre _ray-pohn-druh_
reservation réservation _reh-zehr-vah-see-ohn_
reserve, to réserver _ray-sehr-vay_
reserved réservé _reh-zehr-vay_
resort station _stah-see-ohn_
respond, to répondre _ray-pohn-druh_
return retour _reh-toor_
ribs (cul.) côte _koht_
rice riz _ree_
right (legal) droit _drwah;_ **on the right** à droite _ah drwaht_
ripe mûr(e) _moor_
rise, to lever _leh-vay_
road route _root_
roast/roasted rôti(e) _roh-tee_
roll petit pain _peh-tee payn_
room chambre _sham-bruh_
room temperature température ambiante _tahm-pay-rah-toor ahm-bee-yahnt_
rosemary romarin _roh-mah-rayn_
round rond(e) _rohnd_
rump (of beef) culotte (de bœuf) _koo-loht duh buhf_
runner beans haricots à rames _ah-ree-koh ah rahm_
rural rural(e) _roo-rahl_

safety pin épingle de sécurité ay-*payn*-gluh duh say-koo-ree-*tay*
saffron safran sahf-*frahn*
sage sauge *sohj*
salad salade sah-*lahd*
salmon saumon soh-*mohn*
salt sel *sehl*
salt-cellar salière sahl-ee-*yehr*
salted/salty salé(e) sah-*lay*
same même *mehm*
Saturday samedi sahm-*dee*
sausages saucisses soh-*sees*
savory salé(e) sah-*lay* savoureux sah-voo-*ruh*
say, to dire *deer*
scampi langoustines lahn-goos-*teen*
schedule programme prohgrahm
scour, to frotter froh-*tay*
scrambled eggs œufs brouillés eh broo-ee-*yay*
sea mer *mehr*
sea-bream brème *brehm*
seafood fruits de mer froo-*ee* duh-mehr
seaside bord de la mer bohr-duh-lah-mehr
season saison say-*zohn*
season, to assaisonner ah-say-zohn-*nay*
seasoning assaisonnement ah-say-zohn-*mahn*, condiment kohn-dee-*mahn*
seat siège see-*ehj*
second deuxième duh-zee-ehm
sedative sédatif say-dah-*teef*
see, to voir *vwahr*
sell, to vendre vahn-druh
semolina semoule seh-*mool*
September septembre seh-*tahm*-bruh
set the table, to mettre le couvert *meh*-truh luh koo-vehr
settle, to se déposer suh day-poh-*zay*
shake, to secouer say-koo-*ay*
share part *pahr*
shell coquille koh-*kee*-yuh
shell, to écosser ay-koh-say
shellfish crustacé kroo-stah-say
shop magasin mah-gah-*zayn*
shopping trolley/shopping cart chariot sha-ree-*oh*
shortcrust pastry pâte brisée paht bree-*say*
shoulder épaule ay-*pahl*
show spectacle spehk-*tahk*-luh
show, to montrer mohn-*tray*
sick malade mah-*lahd*
side côté koh-*tay*
simple simple *saym*-pluh

skewer broche *brohsh*,
brochette *broh-sheht*
slice tranche *trahn-shuh*
sliced coupé en tranches
koo-pay ahn trahn-shuh
slip, to glisser *glee-say*
slowly lentement *lahn-teh-mahn*
small petit(e) *peh-tee(t)*
smell odeur *oh-dehr*
smoke, to fumer *foo-may*
smoked fumé(e) *foo-may*
smoked bacon lard fumé *lahr foo-may*
smoked salmon saumon
fumé *soh-mohn foo-may*
smoker fumeur *foo-mehr*
smooth lisse *lees*
snack casse-croûte *kahs-kroot*
snails escargots *ehs-kahr-goh*
soap savon *sah-vohn*
some quelque(s) *kehl-kuh*
somebody quelqu'un *kehl-kuhn*
something quelque chose
kehl-kuh shohz
son fils *fees*
song chanson *shan-shohn*
sorbet/sherbet sorbet *sohr-bay*
soup soupe *soop*
sour aigre *ay-gruh*
sour cherry griotte *gree-oht*

south sud *sood*
soya soja *soh-jah*
sparkling pétillant(e) *pay-tee-yahn(t)*
sparkling water eau gazeuse
oh gah-zehz
spiced/spicy épicé *ay-pee-say*
spices épices *ay-pees*
spinach épinards *ay-pee-nahr*
spit broche *brohsh*
spoon cuillère *kwee-yehr*
square carré *kah-ray*
squid encornet *ahn-kohr-nay*
stairs escalier *ehs-kah-lee-yay*
stamp timbre *taym-bruh*
starch amidon *ah-mee-dohn*
start commencement *koh-mahns-mahn*
start, to commencer *kohm-mahn-say*
station gare *gahr*
stay, to rester *rehs-tay*
steak bifteck *beef-tehk*
steam vapeur *vah-pehr*
stew ragoût *rah-goo*
stewed à l'étouffée *ahl-ay-too-fay*
still encore *ahn-kohr*
still water eau naturale *oh nah-too-rahl*
stomach ache mal à

l'estomac *mahl ahl-ehs-toh-mah*
stop arrêt *ah-reh*
stop, to arrêter *ah-reh-tay*
stopper (bottle) bouchon *boo-shohn*
stout (beer) bière brune *bee-ayr broon*
straight droit *droo-wah*
straight on tout droit *too droo-wah*
strait (sea) détroit *day-twah*
strawberry fraise *frayz*
street rue *roo*
stuffed farci(e) *fahr-see*
stuffing farce *fahrs*
subtle subtil *soob-teel*
such as comme *kuhm*
sugar sucre *soo-kruh*
sugar-bowl sucrier *soo-kree-ay*
sugar-coated almonds dragées *drah-jay*
suitcase valise *vah-leez*
summer été *ay-tay*
summery estival(e) *ehs-tee-vahl*
Sunday dimanche *dee-mahnsh*
supper dîner *dee-nay*
surname nom de famille *nohm-duh-fah-mee-yuh*
surroundings environs *ahn-vee-rohn*

sweet (pastry) sucrerie *soo-kreh-ree*, bonbon *bohn-bohn*; (taste) doux(ce) *doo(s)*
sweetbread ris de veau *ree-duh-voh*
sweetener édulcorant *ay-dool-koh-rahn*
swim, to nager *nah-jay*
swimming pool piscine *pee-seen*
Switzerland Suisse *swees*
swordfish espadon *ehs-pah-dohn*
syrup sirop *see-roh*

tablecloth nappe *nahp*
tablet pastille *pahs-tee-yuh*
tag étiquette *ay-tee-keht*
take, to prendre *prahn-druh*
take away, to emporter *ahm-pohr-tay*
talcum powder talc *tahlk*
tap robinet *roh-bee-nay*
tart tartelette *tahr-teh-leht*
taste goût *goo*
taste, to goûter *goo-tay*
tea thé *tay*
teaspoon petite cuillère *peh-tet kwee-yehr*
telephone call appel téléphonique *ah-pehl tay-lay-foh-neek*
telephone directory annuaire *ah-noo-wayr*

temperature température *tahm-pay-rah-toor*
tender (adj) tendre *tahn-druh*
terminal terminus *tehr-mee-noos*
terrace terrasse *teh-rahs*
thank, to remercier *reh-mehr-see-ay*
thank you remerciement *reh-mehr-see-mahn*
that celui-là, celle-là *seh-loo-ee-lah, sehl-lah*
then ensuite *ahn-soo-weet*
thick épais(se) *ay-peh(s)*
thin mince *mayns*
thing chose *shohz*
thirst soif *soo-wahf*
this celui-ci, celui-là *seh-loo-ee-see, seh-loo-ee-lah*
thousand mille *meel*
thread fil *feel*
throat gorge *gorhj*
throw, to jeter *jeh-tay*
Thursday jeudi *jeh-dee*
thyme thym *taym*
ticket billet *bee-yay*
tie cravate *krah-vaht*
tight serré(e) *sehr-ray*
time temps *tahm*
timetable horaire *oh-rayr*
tin-opener ouvre-boîtes *oo-vruh-boo-waht*
tinned meat viande en

conserve *vee-ahnd ahn kohn-sehrv*
tip pourboire *poor-boo-wahr*
titbits friandise *free-ahn-deez*
toast, to griller *gree-yay*
tobacconist's shop tabac *tah-bah*
today aujourd'hui *oh-joor doo-wee*
together ensemble *ahn-sahm-bluh*
toilet toilettes *too-oh-yuh-leht*
tomato tomate *toh-maht*
tomorrow demain *duh-mayn*
tongue langue *lahn-guh*
tonight ce soir *suh soo-wahr*
too aussi *oh-see*
too much trop *troh*
toothpick cure-dent *kehr-dahn*
tough dur(e) *door*
towards envers, vers *ahn-vehr, vehr*
towel serviette *sehr-vee-eht*
tray plateau *plah-toh*
trout truite *troo-eet*
truffle truffe *troof*
try, to essayer *ehs-say-yay*
Tuesday mardi *mahr-dee*
tunafish thon *tohn*
tureen soupière *soo-pee-ehr*
turkey dinde *daynd*
turn tour *toor*

turn, to tourner *toor-nay*

turn on, to allumer *ah-loo-may*

turn off, to éteindre *ay-tayn-druh*

turned out allumé(e) *ah-loo-may*

turnip navet *nah-vay*

ugly laid(e) *leh(d)*

umbrella parapluie *pah-rah-ploo-ee*

uncomfortable inconfortable *ayn-cohn-fohr-tah-bluh*

uncooked non-cuit(e) *nohn-kwee(t)*

uncork (uncap) déboucher *day-boo-shay*

under sous *soo*

underneath au-dessous *oh-dehs-soo*

understand, to comprendre *kohm-prahn-druh*

United States of America Etats-Unis d'Amérique *eh-tahz oo-nee dah-may-reek*

until jusqu'à *joos-kah*

upbringing éducation *ay dgoo-kah-see-ohn*

use, to utiliser *oo-tee-lee-zay*

V.A.T. T.V.A. *tay-vay-ah*

vacant libre *lee-bruh*

vanilla vanille *vah-nee-yuh*

veal veau *voh*

vegetables légumes *lay-goom;* **raw vegetables** crudités *kroo-dee-tay*

vegetarian végétarien(ne) *vay-jay-tah-ree-ehn(nuh)*

very très *treh*

vinegar vinaigre *vee-nay-gruh*

vitamins vitamines *vee-tah-meen*

wait, to attendre *ah-tahn-druh*

waiter serveur *sehr-vehr*

waitress serveuse *sehr-veehz*

walk, to marcher *mahr-shay*

wall mur *moor*

wallet portefeuille *porh-teh-feh-yuh*

walnuts/nuts noix *noo-wah*

want, to vouloir *voo-loo-whar*

wardrobe garde-robes *gahr-duh-rohb*

warm, to chauffer *shoh-fay*

warn, to prévenir *preh-veh-neer*

wash, to laver *lah-vay*

wasp guêpe *gehp*

watch horloge *ohr-lohj*

watch (look at), to regarder *reh-gahr-day*

water eau *oh*

watermelon pastèque *pahs-tehk*

waterproof imperméable *aym-pehr-may-ah-bluh*

way façon *fah-sohn*

weak faible *feh-bluh*

wear, to porter *pohr-tay*

Wednesday mercredi *mehr-kreh-dee*

week semaine *seh-mehn*

weekday jour ouvrable *joor oo-vrah-bluh*

welcome bienvenu(e) *bee-ehn-veh-noo*

well bien *bee-ehn*

wet (paint) fraîche *frehsh*

What does this mean? Qu'est-ce que cela veut dire ? *kehs-kuh seh-lah vuh deer ?*

What happened? Qu'est-ce que s'est passé ? *kehs-kuh say-pahs-say ?*

what que **kuh**

when quand **kahn**

where où *oo*

whereas alors que *ah-lohr kuh*

which (which one)? quel(le) *kehl*

while pendant *pahn-dahn*

white blanc(he) *blahn(sh)*

who qui *kee*

whole entier *ahn-tee-ay*

wholemeal complet *kohm-pleh*

why pourquoi *poor-koo-wah*

wife femme *fahm*

window fenêtre *feh-neh-truh*

wine vin *vayn*

wine shop marchand de vins, *mahr-chan duh vayn,* cave *kahv*

winter hiver *ee-vehr*

wire fil *feel*

with avec *ah-vehk*

without sans *sahn*

woman femme *fahm*

word mot *moh*

work (mechanism), to marcher *mahr-shay*

write, to écrire *ay-kreer*

year (vintage of a wine) millésimé *mee-lay- see-may*

yeast levure *leh-voor*

yellow jaune *john*

yesterday hier *ee-ayr*

yet (not) pas encore *pahz ahn-kohr*

yoghurt yaourt *yah-oort*

yolk jaune d'œuf *john dehf*

young jeune *jehn*

INDEX